TENNIS

TENNIS

MASTERING THE BASICS WITH THE PERSONALIZED SPORTS INSTRUCTION SYSTEM

Michael Metzler
Georgia State University

Allyn & Bacon
Boston   London   Toronto   Sydney   Tokyo   Singapore

VICE PRESIDENT	Paul A. Smith
Publisher	Joseph E. Burns
EDITORIAL ASSISTANT	Annemarie Kennedy
MARKETING MANAGER	Rick Muhr
EDITORIAL PRODUCTION SERVICE	Bernadine Richey Publishing Services
TEXT DESIGN AND COMPOSITION	Barbara Bert Silbert
MANUFACTURING BUYER	Julie McNeill
COVER ADMINISTRATOR	Brian Gogolin

Copyright ©2001 by Allyn & Bacon
A Pearson Education Company
160 Gould Street
Needham Heights, MA 02494

Internet: www.abacon.com

ISBN: 0-205-32257-3

Printed in the United States of America

10   9   8   7   6   5   4   3   2   1   05   04   03   02   01   00

CONTENTS

PREFACE

INTRODUCTION TO PSIS TENNIS

Hello, and welcome to your **tennis class**! That's right, *your* tennis class. This personal workbook includes almost everything you will need to learn the game of tennis and become a proficient beginning-level player. Of course, your instructor will play an important part as you progress, but most of what you will need is contained in your Personal Workbook. Your tennis class will be taught this term using the **Personalized Sports Instruction System (PSIS)**, developed specifically for college basic instruction courses like the one in which you are enrolled. All of the materials in this workbook have been refined in field tests with many students like yourself, college men and women getting their first formal tennis instruction.

The key design feature of the PSIS is that it permits for individualized learning and progression through the course. Think back to other classes you have taken: some students learn faster than others. This is a fact in all learning situations. Depending on individual learning rates, some students become frustrated if the course goes too fast. Others become bored if the course goes too slowly. Either way, many students become disinterested, reducing their enjoyment of the course. For tennis, the most harmful result of frustration or boredom is that students are not given a proper chance to learn the game and to enjoy it as a regular part of their activity schedule. Whether you are a "bare beginner" or currently have some tennis experience, the PSIS design will allow you to progress **"as quickly as you can, or as slowly as you need."** Keep this little motto in mind as you become familiar with this workbook and progress through your tennis class this term.

Another point to keep in mind is that the PSIS is *achievement oriented*. That means the PSIS design is intended to help you learn the necessary skills, strategies, and rules for beginning tennis play. I guarantee you will be a better player at the end of your PSIS class than you are now!

As you will see, your improvement will come in a way that is different from most other courses you have taken. You will be asked to assume more responsibility for your own learning than ever before. Remember, all the instructional material is included in your Personal Workbook. It will be up to you to learn the contents of the workbook, become familiar with the PSIS system, attend class regularly, follow your instructor's class policies, and work diligently toward completing the course sequences. It has been my experience that college students enjoy taking a large role in their own learning and appreciate the individualized plan of the PSIS. I know that you will, too.

ADVANTAGES OF THE PSIS FOR YOU

1. **The PSIS reduces your dependence on the instructor.** Your Personal Workbook provides nearly all the information you will need to complete the course. All content, learning task, and managerial information is at your fingertips, not with the instructor. When you are ready for a new learning task, the individualized plan will allow you to proceed on your own.
2. **Individualized learning is emphasized.** The PSIS will allow you to learn tennis "as quickly as you can, or as slowly as you need." You will be able to remain in your own comfort zone while progressing through the course.
3. **You will have increased responsibility for your own learning.** As adult learners, college students can assume responsibility for much of their own learning. You can make decisions that have direct bearing on class attendance, practice routines, and achievement. The PSIS system shifts much of the responsibility and decision making directly to you and away from the instructor.
4. **Your access to the instructor will be increased whenever you need it.** Since PSIS instructors can spend much more time in class teaching students, it means that you will get more personal attention and quality instruction, *that is, if you need it.* If you do not require as much interaction with the instructor, it will not be forced on you as with group learning strategies.
5. **You can chart your own progress.** Your PSIS Tennis Personal Workbook includes a simple Personal Progress Chart to help you gauge your learning as you go through the course. This will help you to make decisions about your learning pace, projected grade, and how to use your class time most efficiently.

YOUR ROLE IN PSIS TENNIS

Your role in PSIS Tennis can be summarized easily: become familiar with and follow the Personal Workbook as an independent learning guide. You will not need to depend on the instructor for content and managerial information. But when the workbook is not sufficient or specific learning information is needed, you should be sure to *ASK FOR HELP*! Your Personal Workbook will provide nearly all the information needed to complete the course. So, if you can progress without the instructor's direction, the system is designed to let you. If you need extra help, the instructor will be free to provide it for you. Your instructor will show you a *help signal* for getting his or her attention in class. It might be a raised hand, a raised racquet, or a verbal call. Be sure you know this signal, and do not be shy about using it!

YOUR INSTRUCTOR'S ROLE IN PSIS TENNIS

Your instructor has the important role of *facilitator* in your PSIS tennis course. Your Personal Workbook will provide most of the content and management information you will need, providing your instructor more time to give students individual attention. There will be just one large-group demonstration throughout the entire course, and very little time will be spent organizing routine class "chores." Nearly all the instructor's time will be available to facilitate your learning on an individual basis.

Your instructor has the teaching experience and expertise to make the PSIS work as well as it was designed. The PSIS system allows the instructor to provide the maximum use of his or her expertise by *facilitating* the learning process for you.

SKILL AND KNOWLEDGE COURSE MODULES

Your PSIS tennis course contains a number of learning activities divided into a series of modules. There are two types of modules: **performance skill** and **tennis knowledge**. Performance skill modules focus on the major psychomotor performance patterns needed to play tennis. The tennis knowledge module contains information on basic game rules and tennis etiquette.

PSIS COURSE MANAGEMENT AND POLICIES

In this section you will learn some of the ways in which the PSIS approach can give you increased control over your own learning. Some course management and policies will come from your Personal Workbook. Others will be communicated to you by your instructor. Be sure that you are familiar with all course management routines and policies.

1. **Dressing for class.** You will need to have proper clothing and footwear in order to participate comfortably and safely in your tennis class. We suggest that you wear lightweight, loose-fitting clothes that will not restrict your range of motion (shorts, T-shirts, and the like). General-purpose court shoes or "cross training" shoes with white soles are recommended. Do not wear running shoes or shoes that will make marks on the floor. Specialized clothing and tennis shoes are not necessary. Be sure to ask your instructor about his or her policies regarding dressing for class.

2. **Equipment.** Your instructor will provide you with all the necessary equipment for class, and with the routines for distributing and collecting equipment each day.

3. **Depositing and distributing Personal Workbooks.** Your instructor will advise you on his or her policy regarding your workbook each day after class. We suggest that the instructor collect all student workbooks at the end of class and bring them to class the next day. Be sure that you know the exact policy to be used, since you cannot participate fully in class without your own workbook.

4. **Practice partners.** Some learning tasks will call for you to practice with one or more partners and be checked off by them. Any classmate can be your partner for most tasks. A few tasks will specify that all students in a drill be at the same place in the course learning sequence.

5. **Arriving to class.** Your instructor will inform you about specific routines for arriving to class and beginning each day. Generally, you should (1) arrive at or before the class starting time, (2) locate your own Personal Workbook, (3) complete your stretching and warm-up routine, (4) find a practice partner (if needed at that time), and (5) begin to practice the appropriate learning task. Note that you can begin as soon as you arrive. Except for the first day of instruction, the instructor will not wait to begin the class with all students together. *Arriving before class will allow you extra time to practice your tennis skills.*

6. **Self-checks, partner-checks, and instructor-checks.** Each learning task in PSIS tennis requires that your mastery be documented (checked off). Some tasks can be checked off by you, some must be checked off by a partner, and some by your instructor. Items are checked off by the appropriate person initialing and dating the designated area after each checked

task in your Personal Workbook. Instructor-checked tasks will require that you practice for a period of time prior to attempting mastery and being checked off. When you are ready, indicated by a series of successful trial blocks, signal the instructor and ask him or her to observe you. If you do not reach the stated criterion, you can return for more practice and signal for the instructor again at a later time. *There is no penalty for not making a mastery criterion. You can try as many times as it takes to be successful.* You may find it helpful to alert the instructor at the beginning of a class in which you anticipate needing his or her observation and checking. The instructor will be on the lookout for your signal.

7. **Grading.** Your course instructor will inform you about the grading system and related policies to be used in your PSIS tennis class. Be sure you are aware of the specific requirements and procedures for determining your grade.

USING YOUR TIME EFFECTIVELY

Your PSIS tennis course is made up of a series of predetermined learning tasks grouped into nine modules. Your course will have a set number of class days with a set class length. It is important for you to know your own learning pace and to make steady progress toward completing all course requirements. Therefore, you will need to learn how to best use your time in class and to accurately project completion of PSIS tennis before the end of the term. Here are some helpful tips for managing your time.

1. Arrive to class early and begin right away. No signal will be given by the instructor for class to begin.
2. Stay for the entire class period. Do not get into a habit of leaving early.
3. Learn the PSIS course management system right away. The quicker you understand how it works, the sooner you can start using it to your advantage.
4. Do not hesitate to ask the instructor for assistance. Learn and use the class help signal to get the instructor's attention.
5. If there is not enough time to complete a new task in a class, at least *start* it. This will save time the next day.
6. When you are close to finishing a task at the end of a class, try to stay a few minutes late to complete it. This avoids repetitious setup time the next day and the possible loss of your learning momentum.
7. When a practice partner is needed, pair up with the first person you can find, rather than waiting for a certain person. (This is good way to get to know more of your classmates!)
8. Alert the instructor prior to instructor-checked criterion tasks so that he or she will be available when you need observation and a check-off.

PSIS TENNIS LEARNING MODULES

This section will describe how the PSIS course learning modules are designed. It is important that you know how the PSIS works so that you can take advantage of its individualized learning features. The course learning content is included in two kinds of learning modules: **performance skill** and **tennis knowledge**.

Each *performance skill* module will include the following:

1. A written **introduction** to the skill
2. An **instructor demonstration** of the proper skill techniques
3. Text and photographs that explain the **components** or **phases** of each skill
4. Photographs that highlight the key **performance cues** (these same cues will be presented by the instructor in his or her demonstration).
5. Simple **comprehension tasks** and **readiness drills** to develop initial skill patterns
6. An **error analysis** and **correction section** for self-analyzing common mistakes
7. **Learning tips** for increased proficiency
8. A series of several **criterion tasks** for practicing and demonstrating your skill mastery
9. One or more **challenge tasks** for developing tactical applications of skills in modified competitive situations
10. A **Personal Recording Form** for selected tasks, used to record successful practice trials

The *tennis knowledge* module will include:

1. A **reading** on the basic rules of tennis and tennis game strategy
2. A **knowledge quiz** to test your understanding of the rules and strategy

CHARTING YOUR PROGRESS

The last page of your PSIS tennis workbook includes your **Personal Progress Chart**. Your instructor will show you how to correctly label the chart, and the rest is very simple. At the end of each week in the course, put an x above that date, and across from the last task you completed. As the weeks go by, you will begin to see how your individual learning pace projects your successful completion of all course learning modules.

This introductory section, combined with additional information from your instructor, will allow you to use the PSIS tennis workbook to your full advantage and to learn tennis at your own pace, with highly individualized attention from your instructor. Because PSIS tennis is a complete system for learning the game, it might take you a little time to become familiar with this approach. However, remember that your instructor is there to help when you have questions about the system and when you need individual attention for learning. Now that you know about the PSIS tennis system, you are probably anxious to get started. I hope you enjoy learning tennis with the PSIS approach and that you will become an avid player of this lifelong game. READY...SET...GO!!

STRETCHING FOR TENNIS

INTRODUCTION

Flexibility refers to the ability of the muscles, tendons, and ligaments around a joint to move, while providing support and allowing the joint to move smoothly through its entire range of motion. Increased flexibility means more supple muscles, which reduces the risk of injury to the muscle when the limb is moved suddenly. The static method is the most commonly recommended stretching technique. It has been shown to be extremely effective in increasing range of motion and, when done slowly and carefully, presents little chance of injury to the muscles.

Some sports and forms of exercise lead to improved flexibility of the involved body part. Tennis, for example, tends to limber the shoulder joint and lower back. Gymnastics can only be accomplished with a high degree of flexibility in virtually all points of the body. Activities such as walking and jogging do not require a large range of motion and do not increase flexibility. This is why it is important that stretching should precede these types of exercises. Stretching not only enhances performance, but also reduces the risk of injury.

Flexibility should be included during the warm-up phase of an exercise program. This permits for gentle stretching of muscles around the joint before vigorous movement and leads to a slower cool-down, thereby maintaining local blood flow and reducing postexercise soreness.

Although muscular soreness can have many origins, one major cause appears to be damage to an disruption of the connective tissue elements in the muscles and tendons. No one method of overcoming soreness is available, but adequate stretching appears to aid not only in preventing soreness, but also in relieving it when it already exists.

PERFORMANCE CUES

1. **Warm-up.** Protect the muscle by beginning with a low- to moderate intensity-warm-up for 2 to 3 minutes prior to performing strenuous stretching exercises. Running in place should provide an excellent warm-up.
2. **Do not bounce.** Move into the stretching position slowly, continuing until mild tension is felt. Utilize a static or very slow stretch and hold the position. A ballistic or bouncing stretch can be counterproductive and even cause injury.
3. **Hold the stretch.** The stretch position should be held for a predetermined amount of time. It is suggested that the initial holding position be between 15 and 20 seconds and be gradually increased over the following weeks. As flexibility improves, attempt to hold the stretch slightly longer. When the stretching exercise is complete, the body should be released slowly from the stretch position.
4. **Target zone.** You should not feel pain when stretching a muscle. There is a stretching target zone where *there is tension in the muscle without pain*. It is important to be aware of your own target zone. Stretching at a level below the target zone will not lead to increased flexibility, whereas stretching above this zone will increase the risk of injury.
5. **Breathing.** Do not hold your breath while stretching. Breathing should be slow, rhythmical, and continuous.
6. **Stretch before and after exercise.** Stretching before vigorous exercise prepares the muscles and joints for activity and reduces the risk of injury. Stretching after vigorous exercise is needed to further stretch the muscles. Both warm-up and cool-down are needed.

INSTRUCTOR DEMONSTRATION

Your course instructor will demonstrate each recommended stretching exercise for tennis. Observe the demonstrations carefully, making note of the performance cues for each exercise.

Photo 1.1
Shoulder stretch

Shoulder Stretch (triceps). Elevate one elbow and position the racquet down the middle of your back. Reach behind your back with the other hand and grab the racquet slightly above belt-high. Gently apply force by moving the nonracquet hand down, causing your other elbow to rise (and stretch). Hold the stretch in the target zone for 15 to 20 seconds and slowly release. Repeat this exercise 5 to 8 times with both shoulders. Refer to Photo 1.1.

Lateral Shoulder Stretch. Elevate the arms and grip the racquet at each end. Gently pull down with one arm, stretching the opposite shoulder. Bend your hips in the direction of the pull. Knees should be slightly flexed during the exercise. Hold the stretch in the target zone for 15 to 20 seconds and slowly release. Repeat this exercise 5 to 8 times on both sides of the body. Refer to Photo 1.2.

Photo 1.2
Lateral shoulder stretch

Lower Back and Hamstrings Stretch. From a standing position and holding the racquet at each end, bend forward at the hips and allow the head and arms to hang downward. Have both knees slightly flexed during this exercise. Hold the stretch in the target zone for 15 to 20 seconds and slowly release. Repeat this exercise 5 to 8 times. Refer to Photo 1.3.

Lower Back and Hip Extensor Stretch. From a supine position, elevate one leg toward your chest. Apply pressure for the stretch with both arms pulling toward the chest. Hold the stretch in the target zone for 15 to 20 seconds and slowly release. Repeat this exercise 5 to 8 times with each leg. Refer to Photo 1.4.

Photo 1.3
Lower back and hamstrings stretch

Photo 1.4
Lower back and hip extensor stretch

Photo 1.5
Wall stretch

Wall Stretch (gastrocnemius). Take a position 2 to 3 feet from a wall or solid structure. Lean forward and support your body weight with your forearms. Flex one leg and position the other leg to the rear with the front foot flat on the floor. Force your hips forward while keeping the back leg straight. Hold the stretch in the target zone for 15 to 20 seconds and slowly release. Repeat this exercise 5 to 8 times with each leg. Refer to Photo 1.5.

COMPREHENSION TASK

Partner-Checked

Pair up with another person in the class. In turn, perform each stretch while the other observes for proper technique. Have your partner check and initial below when you have performed each stretch just as your instructor demonstrated. If you have questions or need assistance, use the help signal to alert your instructor.

1. Shoulder stretch
2. Lateral shoulder stretch
3. Lower back and hamstrings stretch
4. Lower back and hip extensor stretch
5. Wall stretch

Partner's initials ————————— Date completed —————————

MODULE

TENNIS BASICS

EQUIPMENT

Tennis requires little equipment to play, one of the reasons for its popularity in so many countries. Tennis equipment is relatively inexpensive and durable. The basic design of the two most essential pieces of equipment, the racquet and the ball, has changed little in several decades. The biggest change has been in the use of lighter and stronger composite materials for the racquet, increasing the power for players of all ability levels. This added power allows today's player to hit shots with greater speed and accuracy, making tennis a much faster game than ever before.

TENNIS RACQUET

The striking implement, or racquet, used to play tennis is lightweight and strong. The body of the racquet is made of a plastic composite material, and the strings are made of thin nylon cord. The handle grip is wrapped with a thin layer of leather. Tennis racquets come in a variety of lengths, weights, grip sizes, head (hitting area) sizes, and tensile strengths. Tensile strength determines how tight the strings can be; the higher the rating, the tighter the racquet can be strung, thus increasing power on the ball.

BALL

The tennis ball comes in a standard size and weight, according to tennis rules. It is hollow, with a rubberlike skin covered with a textured nylon outer coating. Most tennis balls are colored optic yellow to increase visibility.

TENNIS COURT

A tennis court is really two courts in one. One set of lines is used to mark the court for singles play, and an additional set of lines is used to mark the court for doubles play. Illustration 2.1 shows the standard line markings for singles and doubles play. The only difference between the lines for each version is the wider sidelines for doubles, which forms an alley on each side of the court. Both singles and doubles use the same service boxes, baseline, and net.

SHOES AND ATTIRE

It is important that you have the proper shoes for playing tennis to increase both comfort and safety. It is not important at this time to have shoes designed specifically for tennis. Shoes rated for general outdoor court use or cross training will work well. Running shoes are not recommended for tennis, because of their narrow soles and limited ankle support. Finally, make sure your shoes have white, not black, soles so that they will not make marks on the court. Your attire for tennis should include socks, shorts, and a lightweight short-sleeved shirt or t-shirt. Your shorts and shirt should permit for a comfortable, full range of motion and provide good ventilation. Tennis is a very active game and your clothing should allow your body to breathe easily to evaporate perspiration.

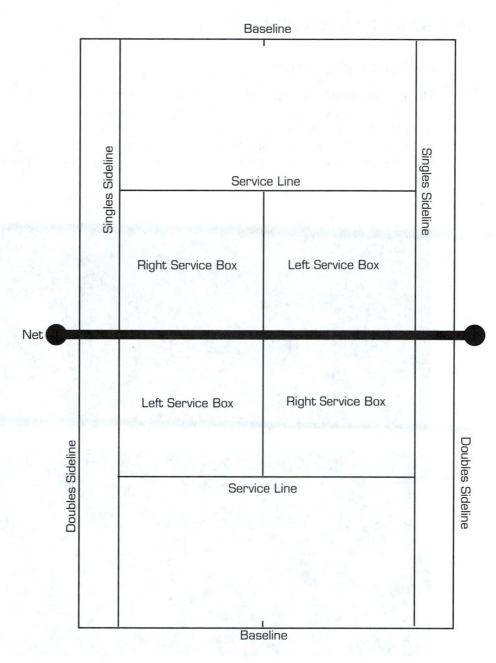

Illustration 2.1
Tennis court, net, and lines

TENNIS STROKE FUNDAMENTALS

GRIPPING THE RACQUET

The grip is a term referring to how the hand fits around the handle of the racquet. There are two basic grips. The Eastern grip is used for forehand shots and serving. The two-hand Continental grip is used for backhand shots. Your grip on the racquet will change according to which shot you are about to hit each time. Refer to Photos 2.1A and B for as you read the following performance cues.

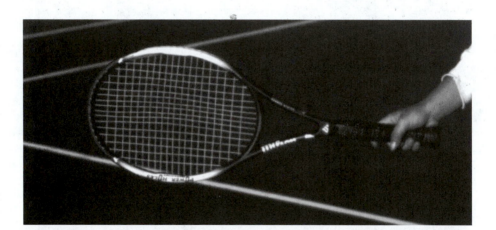

Photos 2.1A and B
Eastern forehand grip

PERFORMANCE CUES FOR FOREHAND GRIP

1. Thumb and index finger form a V which is positioned on top of the grip.
2. Index finger (sometimes called the trigger finger) is wrapped around the grip and separated from the middle finger.
3. Thumb is positioned down and around the grip and is in contact with the middle finger.
4. Heel of the hand is in contact with the base of the grip.
5. Forearm and racquet shaft form an angle of approximately 135 degrees.

COMPREHENSION TASK

Find a partner for this task. Hold the racquet face perpendicular to the court. Have your partner "shake hands" with the grip of the racquet. Use the Performance Cues to decide if his or her forehand grip is correct. Switch roles and repeat this drill. Repeat this drill twice.

READINESS DRILLS

2-1. Assume the Eastern forehand grip. Drop a ball onto the court and, as the ball rebounds, gently hit the ball back to the court. Continue bouncing the ball using the forehand face of the racquet. Your score is the number of times the ball strikes the forehand face of the racquet. Practice this drill until you can keep the ball in play for at least 25 consecutive bounces.

2-2. Assume the Eastern forehand grip. Toss the ball into the air and gently hit it with the racquet. Keep the ball in the air rebounding off the forehand face of the racquet. The score is the number of times the ball strikes the forehand face of the racquet. Practice this drill until you can keep the ball in play for at least 25 consecutive bounces.

2-3. Assume the Eastern forehand grip. Dribble the ball around the court, trying to make the ball bounce on the boundary lines of the court. Practice this drill until you can dribble the ball around the lines of the singles backcourt without losing control of the ball.

Photos 2.2A and B
Two-hand Continental grip (backhand)

Refer to Photos 2.2A and B as you read the performance cues that follow.

PERFORMANCE CUES FOR TWO-HAND BACKHAND GRIP

1. Thumb and index finger form a V which is positioned over the left beveled top edge of the racquet
2. The index finger (sometimes called the trigger finger) is wrapped around the grip and separated from the middle finger.
3. The thumb is positioned down (approximately 45 degrees) and around the grip and is out of contact with the middle finger. The side of the thumb braces the back of the racquet.
4. The heel of the hand is firmly in contact with the base of the handle.
5. Forearm and racquet shaft form an angle of approximately 135 degrees.
6. Nondominant hand is placed firmly on the handle with the palm directly behind the handle.
7. Use your hands as a single unit.

COMPREHENSION TASK

Find a partner for this task. Hold the racquet face perpendicular to the court. Have your partner "shake hands" with the grip of the racquet Use the Performance Cues to decide if his or her backhand grip is correct. Switch roles and repeat this drill. Repeat this drill twice.

READINESS DRILLS

2-4.   Assume the two-hand backhand grip. Drop a ball onto the court and, as the ball rebounds, hit the ball back to the court. Continue bouncing the ball using the backhand face of the racquet. Your score is the number of times the ball strikes the backhand face of the racquet. Practice this drill until you can keep the ball in play for at least 25 consecutive bounces.

2-5.   Assume the two-hand backhand grip. Toss the ball into the air and gently hit it with the racquet. Keep the ball in the air rebounding off the backhand face of the racquet. The score is the number of times the ball strikes the backhand face of the racquet. Practice this drill until you can keep the ball in play for at least 25 consecutive bounces.

2-6.   Assume the two-hand backhand grip. Dribble the ball around the court, trying to make the ball bounce on the boundary lines of the court. Practice this drill until you can dribble the ball around the lines of the singles backcourt without losing control of the ball.

LEARNING TIPS

1. The recommended grip for the forehand is the Eastern. The recommended grip for the backhand is the two-hand backhand (or Continental).
2. Do not "choke-up" on the racquet.
3. Grip the racquet in a firm manner, but not too tight.
4. Relax the grip between strokes.
5. Experiment with slight variations of each grip style.

READY POSITION

The second basic skill in tennis is the ready position, used before and after every shot in a rally and to receive service. The purpose of the ready position is to allow you to move in any direction with equal quickness. Since you cannot know from which direction the ball will come over the net to you, you must be ready to move in any direction. The best way to execute the ready position is to assume a balanced stance, with your weight on the balls of your feet. Refer Photo 2.3 as you read the performance cues for the ready position

Photo 2.3
Ready position

PERFORMANCE CUES

1. **Racquet** the racquet is held in front of the body, midway between the shoulder and knees. the free hand is placed lightly on the throat of the racquet.
2. **Body** weight is evenly distributed on the balls of both feet, the knees are slightly flexed, and the body leans slightly forward from the waist.
3. **Elbows** are held close to the body.
4. **Head** and eyes are to the front, focusing on the ball.

FOOTWORK

You can use the face of a clock to visualize the proper footwork for the ready position, forehand, and backhand shots. Refer to Illustration 2.2, which shows the foot placement for the ready position. The left foot is at 9 o'clock and the right foot is at 3 o'clock (as you look directly down from above the player). Illustration 2.3 shows the foot placement for **forehand** shots (right-handed players). In the correct position for forehand shots, the right (back) foot is at 4 o'clock and the left (front) foot is at 1 o'clock. Illustration 2.4 shows the foot placement for **backhand** shots (right-handed players). In the correct position for backhand shots, the left (back) foot is at 8 o'clock and the right (front) foot is at 11 o'clock.

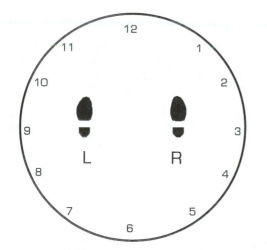

Illustration 2.2
Foot placement for ready position

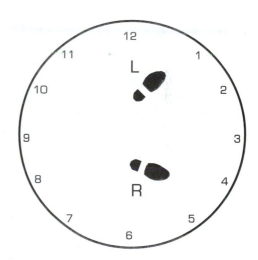

Illustration 2.3
Foot placement for forehand shots

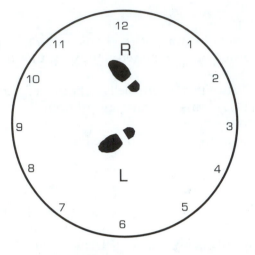

Illustration 2.4
Foot placement for backhand shots

COMPREHENSION TASK

Select a partner and demonstrate the ready position to her or him with all the correct performance cues. While in the correct ready position, have your partner randomly call out "forehand" or "backhand." You should **quickly** execute the correct footwork and grip for the designated shot. Hold your position and have your partner check for correct execution. Be sure to return to the ready position before the next call is made. Do this 10 times and then switch roles with your partner.

READINESS DRILLS

2-7.   Take a ready position in the center of the court just forward of the base-line and face the net (X). Quickly move to the singles sideline by using a side-step pattern (see Illustration 2.5). Keep moving between the side-lines as quickly as possible for at least 20 seconds. Repeat this drill 3

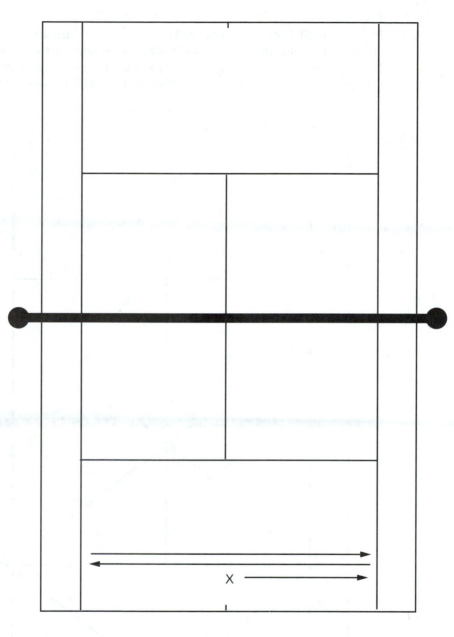

Illustration 2.5
Side-step drill

times.

2-8. Place a small cone or other marker at each of the three court areas shown in Illustration 2.6. Take a ready position in the center of the court just forward of the baseline (X). Face the net and move between the target areas as quickly as possible. Do this drill 3 times using a clock-

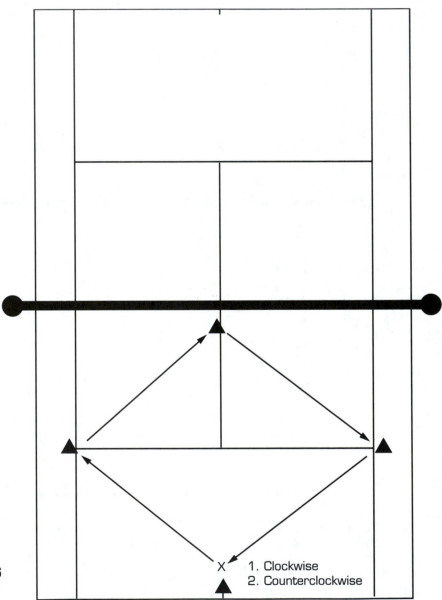

1. Clockwise
2. Counterclockwise

X

Illustration 2.6
Step to targets
drill

wise rotation and 3 times using counterclockwise rotation.

2-9. Assume the ready position approximately 5 to 7 feet behind the baseline (X). Have your court partner (P) stand across the net between the service line and the net and gently toss (underhand) a ball to your forehand side (see Illustration 2.7). Move to the ball and prepare to stroke the ball on the first bounce. **Do not actually hit the ball. Repeat this**

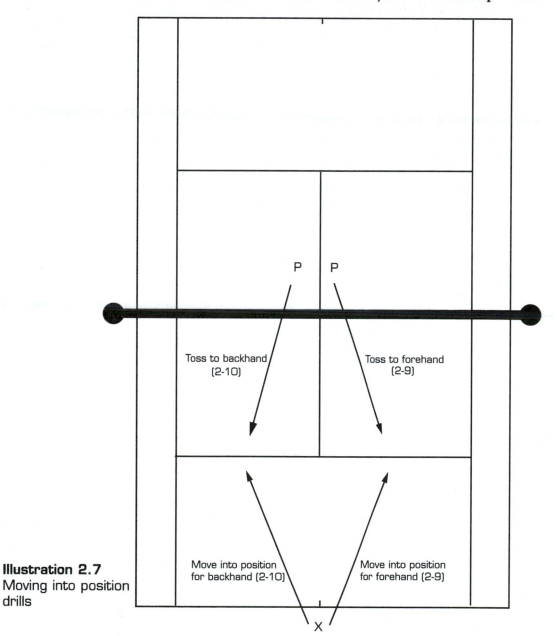

P   P

Toss to backhand
(2-10)

Toss to forehand
(2-9)

Move into position
for backhand (2-10)

Move into position
for forehand (2-9)

X

Illustration 2.7
Moving into position
drills

drill 10 times.

2-10. Assume the ready position approximately 5 to 7 feet behind the baseline (X). Have your court partner (P) stand across the net between the service line and the net and gently toss (underhand) a ball to your backhand side (see Illustration 2.7 again). Move to the ball and prepare to stroke the ball on the first bounce. **Do not actually hit the ball.** Repeat this drill 10 times.

MODULE 3

GROUND STROKES

INTRODUCTION

Ground strokes are executed by the player striking the ball as it bounces off the court, usually from the area behind the baseline. There are two basic ground strokes. The forehand drive is hit with the ball on the player's dominant-hand side and is the most dependable and powerful shot for all players. The backhand drive shot is hit with the ball on the player's nondominant side, making it a somewhat weaker shot for most players. The ability to hit crisp and accurate ground strokes is the most basic requirement for becoming a proficient tennis player.

FOREHAND DRIVE

INSTRUCTOR DEMONSTRATION

Your course instructor will provide you with an explanation and demonstration of the key performance cues for the forehand drive. If you have questions, be sure to ask them before proceeding to the individualized task sequence. The basic forehand drive involves three phases: **preparation** (preparing to stroke the ball), **contact** (contacting the ball) and follow-through (stroke pattern after ball contact). Refer to Photos 3.1A through C as your instructor explains and demonstrates each performance cue for the forehand drive.

Photo 3.1A
Preparation phase

Photo 3.1B
Contact phase

Photo 3.1C
Follow-through phase

PERFORMANCE CUES FOR PREPARATION PHASE

1. **Grip:** Eastern forehand grip.
2. **Backswing:** Shoulder level.
3. **Body rotation:** Hip and shoulders rotate, placing the side of the body toward the net.

PERFORMANCE CUES FOR CONTACT PHASE

4. **Weight transfer:** From back foot to front foot.
5. **Forward swing:** Upward to meet the approaching ball.
6. **Ball contact:** Just forward of the lead foot.

PERFORMANCE CUES FOR FOLLOW THROUGH PHASE

7. **Body rotation:** Hip and shoulders rotate fully, positioning the front of the body toward the net.
8. **Forward swing:** Upward across the body, ending above the level of the head.

COMPREHENSION TASK

Find a partner and demonstrate to each other the proper performance cues for the forehand shot *without hitting the ball.* Start out with slow, deliberate strokes. Be sure to provide feedback to each other for correct and incorrect performance cues until both of you can execute this shot correctly.

LEARNING TIPS

1. The recommended grip for the forehand is the Eastern. You can experiment with slightly different hand positioning to "customize" your grip for this shot.
2. Always start from the ready position and change to the proper grip before you begin your swing.
3. When you take the racquet back, make sure that your hips and shoulders rotate to position your side to the approaching ball.
4. When executing the foot pivot, shift your body weight to your rear foot.
5. Use a loop swing, not straight backward and forward.
6. The head of the racquet should be below the approaching ball as the racquet moves toward point of contact.
7. Take a step forward to contact the approaching ball and make sure your body weight shifts from back foot to front foot.
8. At the point of ball impact, keep the wrist firm to minimize vibration.
9. Racquet follow-through is across your body and elevated.

READINESS DRILLS

3-1. Find a spot in the practice area, facing a fence or hitting wall. Stand about 20 feet from the fence. While always starting from the ready position, bounce the ball to yourself and gently hit 50 forehand drives into the fence. Do not be concerned with a specific aiming area at this time. Use these shots to gauge the proper timing, feel, and contact point for the forehand drive shot. *Remember, hit gentle shots.*

3-2. Take a position behind the baseline with your nondominant side toward the net. Gently drop a ball onto the court on your forehand side. As the ball bounces from the court, stroke it over the net with a forehand drive. Your objective is to just get the ball over the net, landing anywhere in the opposite doubles court area. Do not be concerned with hitting the ball hard at this time. Do this until you have hit 50 successful forehand drives.

3-3. You will need a partner for this drill. Assume the ready position approximately 5 to 7 feet behind the baseline (X). Have your partner (P) stand close to the net on your side of the court and gently toss (underhand) balls to your forehand side. Move to the ball and stroke it on the first bounce. Your objective is to just get the ball over the net, landing anywhere in the opposite doubles court area (see Illustration 3.5). Do not be concerned with hitting the ball hard at this time. Do this until you have hit 50 successful forehand drives.

If you experiencing difficulty with the readiness drills, refer to the **performance cues** and review each cue as presented. If you still have difficulty, ask your course instructor to assist you in applying these techniques.

Common Errors and Their Correction

Error	Correction
Pushing the ball. It goes to the right on a straight line.	1. Adjust contact point more to the front. 2. Adjust body contact point a bit farther from your body.
Pulling the ball. It goes to the left on a straight line.	1. Adjust contact point more to the back. 2. Adjust contact point a bit farther from your body.
Ball goes into the net.	1. Shift body weight forward into the ball. 2. Increase hip and shoulder rotation. 3. Open the face of the racquet prior to ball contact.
Ball travels over the baseline or goes too high.	1. Close face of the racquet at contact prior to ball contact. 2. Be sure your body weight comes forward with the racquet. Do not hit with your weight on your back foot.

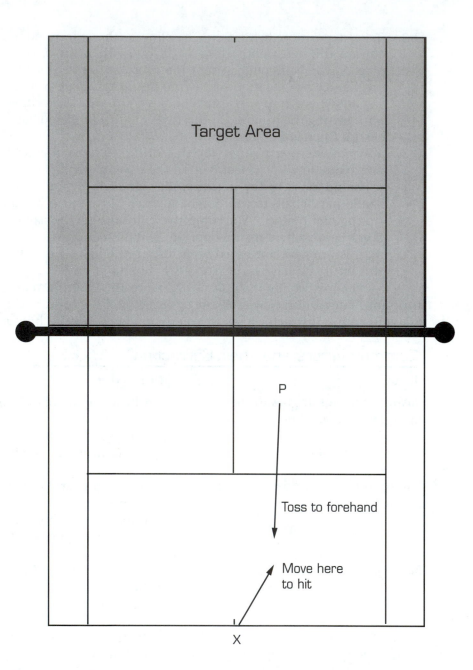

Illustration 3.1
Forehand readiness drill

CRITERION TASK 3-1

Partner-Checked

Assume the ready position just behind the baseline (X). Have your partner (P) stand close to the net on your side of the court and gently toss (underhand) balls to your forehand side. Move to the ball and stroke it on the first bounce. The ball must land within the court area bounded by the singles sidelines, the service line, and the baseline (see Illustration 3.2). Play all tosses with a forehand drive. If your partner's toss is not accurate, still make an attempt to hit it. If you are not successful on an errant toss, do not count that one. Practice this task in blocks of 10 shots. Record the number of successful shots for each block on the **Personal Recording Form**. When four block scores reach or exceed 7 out of 10 (they do not have to be consecutive), have your partner initial and date in the space provided.

Personal Recording Form									
Block 1	Block 2	Block 3	Block 4	Block 5	Block 6	Block 7	Block 8	Block 9	Block 10
___/10	___/10	___/10	___/10	___/10	___/10	___/10	___/10	___/10	___/10

Your partner's initials _____   Date completed _____

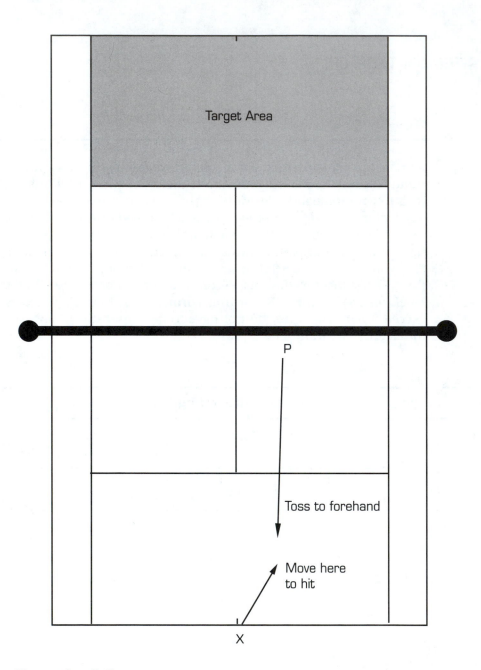

Illustration 3.2
Criterion Task 3-1

CRITERION TASK 3-2

Partner-Checked

Assume a ready position just behind the baseline (X).Have your court partner take a position directly across the net (P) and hit gentle shots to your fore-hand side. The target area is defined by the service line, singles sideline, base-line, and service area divider line (extended to the baseline) on the side of the opposite court that your partner is standing in (see Illustration 3.3). If your partner's shot to you is not accurate, still make an attempt to hit it. If you are not successful on an errant shot, do not count that one. Practice this task in blocks of 10 shots. Record the number of successful shots for each block on the **Personal Recording Form**. When four block scores reach or exceed 7 out of 10 (they do not have to be consecutive), have your partner initial and date in the space provided.

Personal Recording Form									
Block 1	Block 2	Block 3	Block 4	Block 5	Block 6	Block 7	Block 8	Block 9	Block 10
___/10	___/10	___/10	___/10	___/10	___/10	___/10	___/10	___/10	___/10

Your partner's initials _____ Date completed _____

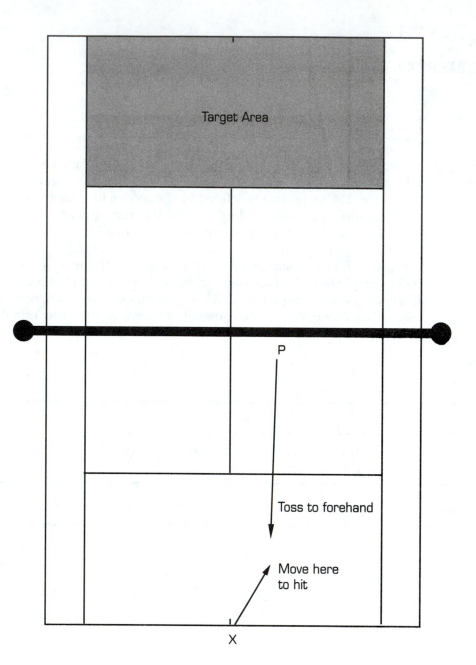

Illustration 3.3
Criterion Task 3-2

BACKHAND DRIVE

To become a good tennis player, you must develop the ability to stroke the ball with authority using both the forehand and backhand. However, in the early stages of learning, many players develop an irrational fear of the backhand stroke. As a result, the backhand is often exploited during competition. Given the proper information and sufficient practice, you can develop a backhand that is both consistent and aggressive.

INSTRUCTOR DEMONSTRATION

Your course instructor will provide you with an explanation and demonstration of the key performance cues for the backhand drive. If you have questions, be sure to ask them before proceeding to the individualized task sequence. The basic backhand drive involves three phases: **preparation** (preparing to stroke the ball), **contact** (contacting the ball) and **follow-through** (stroke pattern after ball contact). Refer to Photos 3.2A through C as your instructor explains and demonstrates each performance cue for the backhand drive.

Photo 3.2A
Preparation phase

PERFORMANCE CUES FOR PREPARATION PHASE

1. **Grip:** Two-hand backhand grip.
2. **Backswing:** Shoulder level
3. **Body rotation:** Hip and shoulders rotate, placing the side of the body toward the net.

Photo 3.2B
Contact phase

Photo 3.2C
Follow-through phase

PERFORMANCE CUES FOR CONTACT PHASE

4. **Weight transfer:** From back foot to front foot.
5. **Forward swing:** Upward to meet the approaching ball.
6. **Ball contact:** Just forward of the lead foot.

PERFORMANCE CUES FOR FOLLOW THROUGH PHASE

7. **Body rotation:** Hip and shoulders fully rotate, positioning the front of the body toward the net.
8. **Forward swing:** Upward across the body, ending above the level of the head.

COMPREHENSION TASK

Find a partner and demonstrate to each other the proper performance cues for the backhand drive shot *without hitting the ball*. Start out with slow, deliberate strokes. Be sure to provide feedback to each other for correct and incorrect performance cues until both of you can execute this shot correctly.

LEARNING TIPS

1. The recommended grip for the backhand is the two-handed (Continental) grip.
2. Always start from the ready position and change to the proper grip before you begin your backswing.
3. When you take the racquet back, make sure that your hips and shoulders rotate to position your side to the approaching ball.
4. When executing the foot pivot, shift your body weight to your rear foot.
5. Use a loop swing, not straight backward and forward.
6. The head of the racquet should be below the approaching ball as the racquet moves toward point of contact.
7. Take a step forward to contact the approaching ball and make sure your body weight shifts from back foot to front foot.
8. At the point of ball impact, keep the wrists firm to reduce vibration.
9. Follow-through is across your body and elevated, with two hands on the racquet.

READINESS DRILLS

3-4. Find a spot in the practice area, facing a fence or hitting wall. Stand about 20 feet from the fence. While always starting from the ready position, bounce the ball to yourself and gently hit 50 backhand drives into the fence. Do not be concerned with a specific aiming area at this time. Use these shots to gauge the proper timing, feel, and contact point for the backhand drive shot. *Remember, hit gentle shots.*

3-5. Take a position behind the baseline with your dominant side toward the net. Gently drop a ball onto the court on your backhand side. As the ball bounces from the court, stroke it over the net with a backhand drive. Your objective is to just get the ball over the net, landing anywhere in the opposite doubles court area. Do not be concerned hitting the ball hard at this time. Do this until you have hit 50 successful backhand drives.

3-6. You will need a partner for this drill. Assume the ready position just behind the baseline (X). Have your partner stand close to the net on your side of the court (P) and gently toss (underhand) balls to your backhand side. Move to the ball and stroke it on the first bounce. Your objective is to just get the ball over the net, landing anywhere in the opposite doubles court area (see Illustration 3.4). Do not be concerned with hitting the ball hard at this time. Do this until you have hit 50 successful backhand drives.

If you experience difficulty with the readiness drills, refer to the **performance cues** and review each cue as presented. If you still have difficulty, ask your course instructor to assist you in applying these techniques.

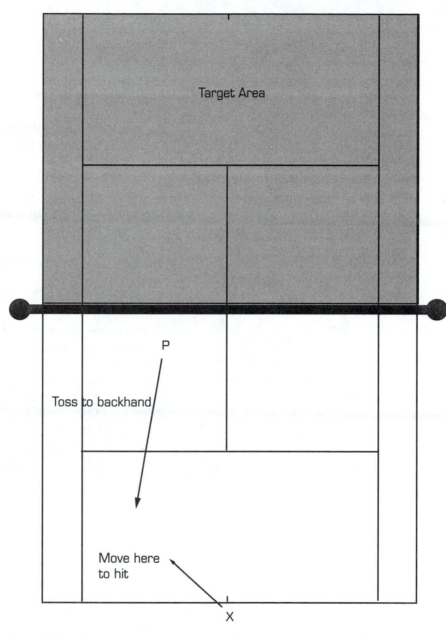

Target Area

P

Toss to backhand

Move here
to hit

X

Illustration 3.4
Backhand Readiness Drill 3-4

Common Errors and Their Correction

Error	Correction
Pushing the ball. It goes to the left on a straight line.	1. Adjust contact point more to the front. 2. Adjust contact point a bit farther from your body.
Pulling the ball. It goes to the right on a straight line.	1. Adjust contact point more to the back. 2. Adjust contact point a bit farther from your body.
Ball goes into the net.	1. Shift body weight forward into the ball. 2. Increase hip and shoulder rotation. 3. Open the face of the racquet prior to ball contact.
Ball travels over the baseline or goes too high.	1. Close face of the racquet at contact prior to ball contact. 2. Be sure your body weight comes forward with the racquet. Do not hit with your weight on your back foot.

CRITERION TASK 3-3

Partner-Checked

Assume the ready position just behind the baseline (X). Have your partner (P) stand close to the net on your side of the court and gently toss (under-hand) balls to your backhand side. Move to the ball and stroke it on the first bounce. The ball must land within the court area bounded by the sin-gles sidelines and to the rear of the service line (see Illustration 3.5). Play all tosses with a backhand drive. If your partner's toss is not accurate, still make an attempt to hit it. If you are not successful on an errant toss, do not count that one. Practice this task in blocks of 10 shots. Record the number of successful shots for each block on the Personal Recording Form. When four block scores reach or exceed 7 out of 10 (they do not have to be consecutive), have your partner initial and date in the space provided.

Personal Recording Form									
Block 1	Block 2	Block 3	Block 4	Block 5	Block 6	Block 7	Block 8	Block 9	Block 10
___/10	___/10	___/10	___/10	___/10	___/10	___/10	___/10	___/10	___/10

Your partner's initials _____   Date completed _____

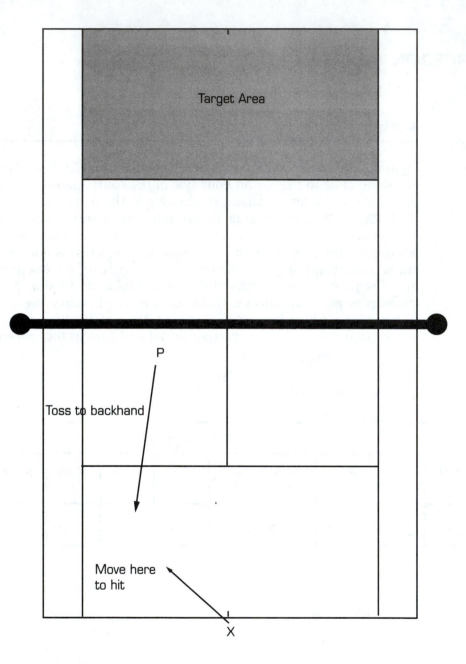

Illustration 3.5
Criterion Task 3-3

CRITERION TASK 3-4

Partner-Checked

Assume a ready position just behind the baseline (X). Have your partner take a position directly across the net (P) and hit gentle shots to your backhand side. The target area is defined by the short service line, singles sideline, baseline, and service area divider line (extended to the baseline) on the side of the opposite court that your partner is standing in (see Illustration 3.6). If your partner's shot to you is not accurate, still make an attempt to hit it. If you are not successful on an errant shot, do not count that one. Practice this task in blocks of 10 shots. Record the number of successful shots for each block on the **Personal Recording Form.** When four block scores reach or exceed 7 out of 10 (they do not have to be consecutive), have your partner initial and date in the space provided.

Personal Recording Form									
Block 1	Block 2	Block 3	Block 4	Block 5	Block 6	Block 7	Block 8	Block 9	Block 10
___/10	___/10	___/10	___/10	___/10	___/10	___/10	___/10	___/10	___/10

Your partner's initials _____   Date completed _____

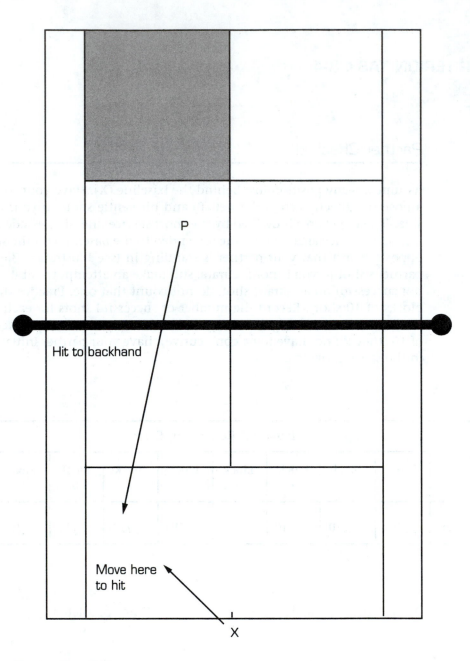

Illustration 3.6
Criterion Task 3-4

CHALLENGE TASK

You will need a partner for this task. You will be positioned just behind one baseline, your partner will be positioned just behind the opposite baseline. The objective is to complete a rally of 20 consecutive forehand or backhand drive shots. For a shot to count, it must: (1) be struck on the first bounce, (2) land in the opposite singles area, and (3) be deep enough so that the returner can hit the ball while remaining behind the baseline. The idea is to hit shots with good control and accuracy so that your partner can return them easily. Remember, you are both on the same team! Complete this task with two different partners.

MODULE 4

APPROACH SHOTS

INTRODUCTION

Tennis players practice both the forehand and backhand drives in concert to develop a balanced game. The previous ground stroke module was oriented toward proper stroke production with limited movement to the ball. The game of tennis however, requires players to develop a combination of quick movement, sound footwork, and efficient stroke mechanics. Proper footwork begins with the baseline game, in which a player executes a series of forehand and backhand drives while moving from side to side. Tennis players must also learn the forward footwork involved when attacking the net. These are called approach shots, based on a sequence of anticipation, movement to the ball, timing, and stroke mechanics.

INSTRUCTOR DEMONSTRATION

Your course instructor will provide you with an explanation and demonstration of the key performance cues for the forehand and backhand approach shots. If you have questions, be sure to ask them before proceeding to the individualized task sequence. *As you will note, these shots use the same mechanics as their respective ground strokes, once you have moved into the proper position to make a shot.*

LEARNING TIPS

1. Attempt to get into the ready position before your opponent hits her or his shot
2. Be sure to assume the proper grip once you have decided to hit a forehand or backhand shot.

3. Move to the ball as you take the racquet back. Make sure that your hips and shoulders rotate to position your side to the approaching ball.
4. As you reach the anticipated point of ball contact, plant your rear foot and shift your body weight forward into the stroke.
5. The head of the racquet should be below the approaching ball as the racquet moves toward point of contact.
6. At the point of ball impact, keep the wrist firm. Use a strong follow-through across your body and elevated.
7. When attempting an approach shot, take the racquet halfway back as you move to the anticipated ball contact.
8. Always return to the ready position when you have completed each shot.
9. Be patient! Approach shots involve many variables and minute changes as you move to stroke the ball. The necessary timing and decision-making skills require many practice attempts to master.

READINESS DRILLS

4-1. Assume a position behind the baseline (X). Have your court partner assume a position across the net (P) and gently toss the ball (underhand) to your forehand side, deep enough so that you must move laterally. Move to the ball, execute the proper ground stroke and drive the ball over the net into the singles court area (see Illustration 4.1). Practice from the forehand side until you have hit 25 successful shots. Next, have your court partner toss the ball to your backhand side. Move laterally to the ball and drive it over the net into the singles court area. Be sure to make the appropriate grip changes. Practice from the backhand side until you have hit 25 successful shots.

4-2. Assume a position behind the baseline (X). Have your court partner assume a position across the net (P) and gently toss the ball (underhand) to your forehand side. The ball should land near the back of the service line. Move forward to the ball and execute the proper approach shot, aiming for the opposite singles court area (see Illustration 4.1 again). Practice from the forehand side until you have hit 25 successful shots. Next, have your court partner toss the ball to your backhand side. Execute an approach shot and stroke the ball over the net into the singles court area. Practice from the backhand side until you have hit 25 successful shots. Be sure to make the appropriate grip changes.

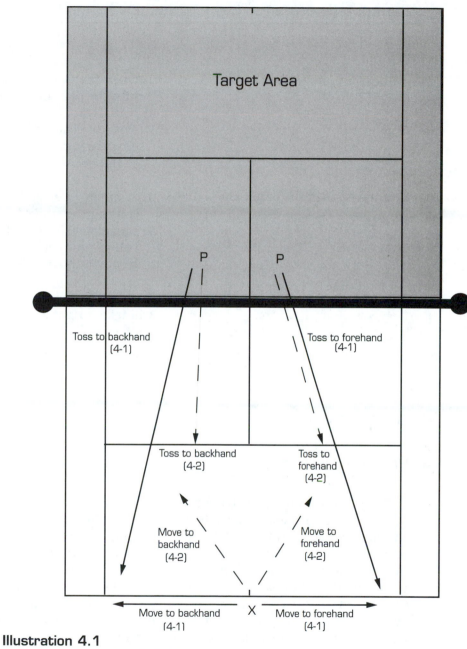

Illustration 4.1
Readiness Drills 4-1 and 4-2

Common Errors and Their Correction

Error	Correction
Ball travels into the net.	1. Open the face of the racquet into the net prior to ball contact. 2. Flex knees and drop the head of racquet during the approach to the net.
Ball travels over the baseline.	1. "Gather" yourself before starting the stroke. 2. Move quickly enough to the ball so that you can get your back foot planted early.
Ball hits the rim of the racquet.	Anticipate where the ball's flight will take it right at the point of contact and be ready for it.

CRITERION TASK 4-1

Partner-Checked

Take a position behind the baseline with your side toward the net (X). Have your court partner assume a ready position behind the baseline on the opposite side of the net (P). Gently drop a ball onto the court on your forehand side, and stroke it over the net to either side of the playing court. Your partner will return the ball with the appropriate ground stroke. Your objective is to return that shot back over the net into the opposite singles area (see Illustration 4.2). If your partner's shot to you is not accurate, still make an attempt to hit it. If you are not successful on an errant shot, do not count that one. Practice this task in blocks of 10 shots. Record the number of successful shots for each block on the **Personal Recording Form**. When four block scores reach or exceed 7 out of 10 (they do not have to be consecutive), have your partner initial and date in the space provided.

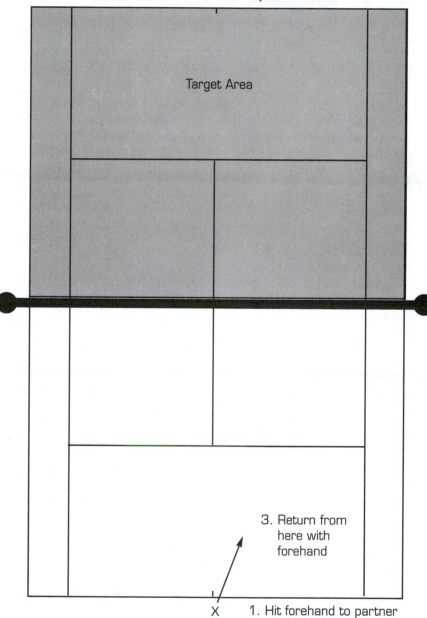

P   2. Partner returns to
          your forehand

Target Area

3. Return from
   here with
   forehand

X   1. Hit forehand to partner

Illustration 4.2
Criterion Task 4-1

Personal Recording Form									
Block 1	Block 2	Block 3	Block 4	Block 5	Block 6	Block 7	Block 8	Block 9	Block 10
__/10	__/10	__/10	__/10	__/10	__/10	__/10	__/10	__/10	__/10

Your partner's initials _____   Date completed _____

CRITERION TASK 4-2

Partner-Checked

Take a position behind the baseline with your side toward the net (X). Have your court partner assume a ready position behind the baseline on the opposite side of the net (P). Gently drop a ball onto the court on your forehand side, and stroke it over the net to either side of the playing court. Your partner will return the ball with the appropriate ground stroke to your forehand side. Your objective is to return that shot back over the net in an area defined by the service line, the singles sideline, the baseline, and the service divider line (extended) on your partner's forehand side (see Illustration 4.3). If your partner's shot to you is not accurate, still make an attempt to hit it. If you are not successful on an errant shot, do not count that one. Practice this task in blocks of 10 shots. Record the number of successful shots for each block on the **Personal Recording Form.** When four block scores reach or exceed 7 out of 10 (they do not have to be consecutive), have your partner initial and date in the space provided.

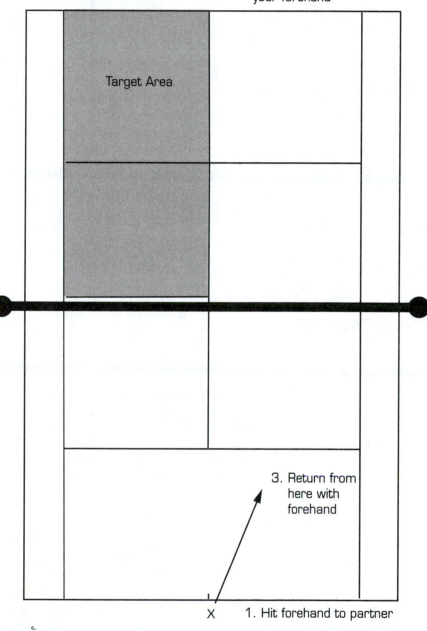

P 2. Partner returns to your forehand

Target Area

3. Return from here with forehand

X 1. Hit forehand to partner

Illustration 4.3
Criterion Task 4-2

Personal Recording Form									
Block 1	Block 2	Block 3	Block 4	Block 5	Block 6	Block 7	Block 8	Block 9	Block 10
__/10	__/10	__/10	__/10	__/10	__/10	__/10	__/10	__/10	__/10

Your partner's initials _____   Date completed _____

CRITERION TASK 4-3

Partner-Checked

Take a position behind the baseline with your side toward the net (X). Have your court partner assume a ready position behind the baseline on the opposite side of the net (P). Gently drop a ball onto the court on your forehand side, and stroke it over the net to either side of the playing court. Your partner will return the ball with the appropriate ground stroke to your backhand side. Your objective is to return that shot back over the net in an area defined by the service line, the singles sideline, the baseline, and the service divider line (extended) on your partner's backhand side (see Illustration 4.4). If your partner's shot to you is not accurate, still make an attempt to hit it. If you are not successful on an errant shot, do not count that one. Practice this task in blocks of 10 shots. Record the number of successful shots for each block on the **Personal Recording Form**. When four block scores reach or exceed 7 out of 10 (they do not have to be consecutive), have your partner initial and date in the space provided.

P

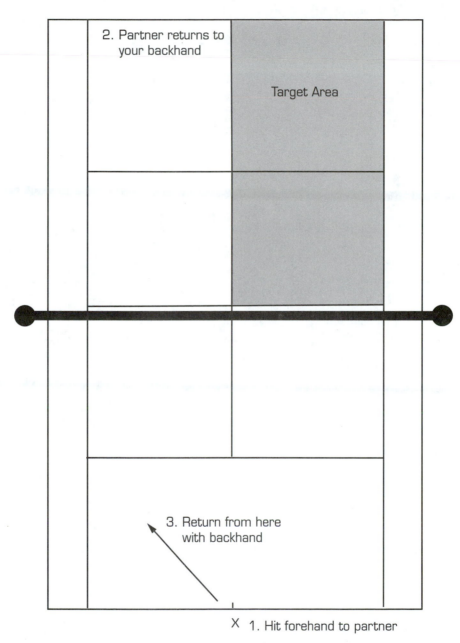

2. Partner returns to
your backhand

Target Area

3. Return from here
with backhand

X 1. Hit forehand to partner

Illustration 4.4
Criterion Task 4-3

VOLLEYS

INTRODUCTION

The approach shots you just learned can be used to begin an aggressive, attacking strategy in tennis. Once you have made an approach shot that gets you moving forward toward the net, you are faced with a key decision: do I keep going to the net, or do I drop back to hit another ground stroke? "Going to the net" indicates that you are on the attack and, once there, requires the use of the volley shot. On a volley the ball is struck in your court without first letting it bounce. Most volleys are struck between the service line and the net. In fact, there is a strategic territory, called "no man's land," just behind the service line, extending back about 15 feet. You should never take up a ready position in that area of the court because most balls coming to you there will bounce near your feet, making them difficult to handle. Be decisive; either hit an approach shot and go all the way to net anticipating a volley, or stay behind "no man's land" and set up for a ground stroke return. *Due to the nature of tennis doubles, volleying is one of the key strokes used in that version of the game, so you must master these shots to be ready for doubles play.*

FOREHAND VOLLEY

INSTRUCTOR DEMONSTRATION

Your course instructor will provide you with an explanation and demonstration of the key performance cues for the forehand volley shot. If you have questions, be sure to ask them before proceeding to the individualized task sequence. As you will note, the backswing and the follow-through are severely shortened and top spin is not used. There is a premium on placement, not on speed or spin. The forehand volley involves three phases: **preparation** (preparing to stroke the ball), **contact** (contacting the ball) and **follow-through** (stroke pattern after ball contact). Refer to Photos 5.1A through C as your instructor explains and demonstrates each performance cue for the forehand drive.

PERFORMANCE CUES FOR PREPARATION PHASE
(note position on the court)

1. **Grip:** Eastern forehand grip.
2. **Knees:** Slightly flexed, ready for a short, quick step in either direction.

Photo 5.1A
Forehand volley, preparation phase

Photo 5.1B
Forehand volley, contact phase

Photo 5.1C
Forehand volley,
follow-through phase

PERFORMANCE CUES FOR CONTACT PHASE

3. **Weight transfer:** Forward toward front foot.
4. **Ball contact:** Even with or slightly forward of the front foot.

PERFORMANCE CUES FOR FOLLOW-THROUGH PHASE

5. **Body rotation:** Hip and shoulders rotate slightly toward the net.
6. **Forward swing:** Continues toward the net with a short follow-through.

COMPREHENSION TASK

Find a partner and demonstrate to each other the proper performance cues for the forehand volley shot *without hitting the ball*. Start with slow, deliberate strokes. Be sure to provide feedback to each other for correct and incorrect performance cues until both of you can execute this shot correctly.

LEARNING TIPS

1. Always start from the ready position, close to the net.
2. Keep the elbows in close and slightly in front of the body.
3. Be ready to change your grip as soon as you decide which side to hit from.
4. The knees are flexed and the body weight is on the balls of the feet.
5. Immediately upon determining on which side the ball is approaching, use hip and shoulder rotation to initiate your body pivot.
6. Use very little backswing; no farther than even with the hitting shoulder.
7. Shift body weight from back to front as you initiate the forward swing.
8. The head of the racquet should be above the approaching ball as the racquet moves toward point of contact.
9. The forward swing is a punching or blocking motion. At the point of ball impact, keep the wrist firm.
10. The follow-through is relatively short (approximately 12 to 15 inches past ball impact).

READINESS DRILLS

5-1. Find a spot in the practice area facing a fence or hitting wall. Stand about 10 feet from the fence. While always starting from the ready position, bounce the ball to yourself and gently hit 50 forehand volley shots into the fence. Do not be concerned with a specific aiming area at this time. Use these shots to gauge the proper timing, feel, and contact point for this shot. *Remember, hit gentle shots.*

5-2. Take a position near the net with your nondominant side toward the net. Gently drop a ball onto the court on your forehand side. As the ball bounces from the court, stroke it over the net with a forehand volley. Your objective is to just get the ball over the net, landing anywhere in the opposite doubles court area. Do not be concerned with accuracy at this time. Do this until you have hit 50 successful forehand volleys.

5-3. You will need a partner for this drill. Assume the ready position approximately 6 to 8 feet behind the net (X). Have your partner stand just inside the service line on the other side of the court (P), slightly off to your forehand side, and gently toss (underhand) balls to your forehand side. Move to the ball and stroke it before it hits the court. Your objective is to just get the ball over the net, landing anywhere in the opposite doubles court area (see Illustration 5.5). Do not be concerned with hitting the ball hard at this time. Do this until you have hit 50 successful forehand volleys.

If you are experiencing difficulty with the readiness drills, refer to the **performance cues** and review each cue as presented. If you still have difficulty, ask your course instructor to assist you in applying these techniques.

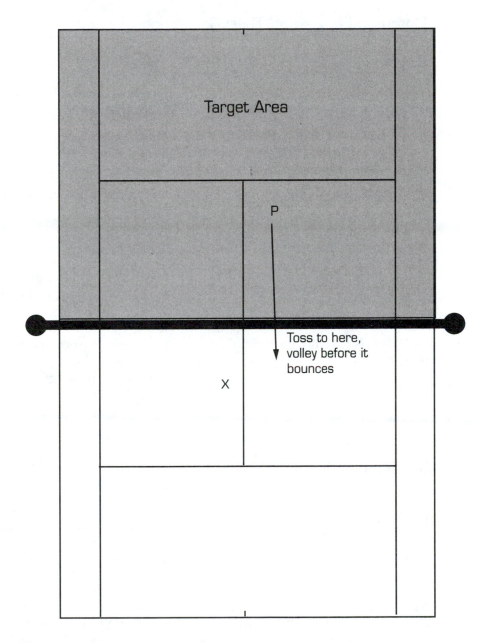

Target Area

P

Toss to here,
volley before it
bounces

X

Illustration 5.1
Readiness Drill 5-3

Common Errors and Their Correction

Error	Correction
No power on the volleys.	1. Anticipate and be ready. 2. Transfer body weight to front foot. 3. Make contact just forward of front foot.
Balls goes into the net.	1. Flex knees to get your body low. 2. Open the racquet face prior to contact.
Racquet turns in hand at contact.	1. Check for proper grip. 2. Keep your wrist locked and firm through contact.
Ball travels over the baseline or goes too high.	1. Close face of the racquet at contact. 2. Shorten the length of your stroke.

CRITERION TASK 5-1

Partner-Checked

Take a ready position close to the net. Have your court partner take a position across the net in the area between the service line and the baseline (X). Your court partner executes a medium-speed forehand drive to your forehand. Return his shot with a forehand down-the-line volley. The ball must land in the target area defined by the service line, the singles sideline, the baseline, and the service divider line (extended) on your partner's backhand side (directly upcourt from you) (see Illustration 5.2). If your partner's shot to you is not accurate, still make an attempt to hit it. If you are not successful on an errant shot, do not count that one.

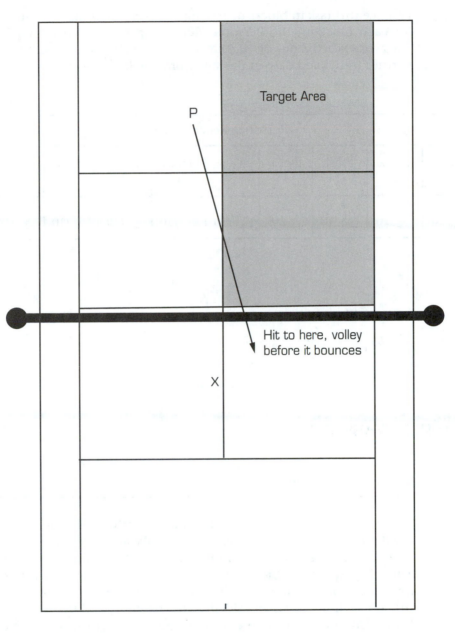

Target Area

P

Hit to here, volley
before it bounces

X

Illustration 5.2
Criterion Task 5-1

Practice this task in blocks of 10 shots. Record the number of successful shots for each block on the **Personal Recording Form**. When four block scores reach or exceed 7 out of 10 (they do not have to be consecutive), have your partner initial and date in the space provided.

Personal Recording Form									
Block 1	Block 2	Block 3	Block 4	Block 5	Block 6	Block 7	Block 8	Block 9	Block 10
___/10	___/10	___/10	___/10	___/10	___/10	___/10	___/10	___/10	___/10

Your partner's initials _____   Date completed _____

CRITERION TASK 5-2

Partner-Checked

Take a ready position close to the net, slightly to the right of the service divider line (X). Have your court partner take a position across the net in the area between the service line and the baseline (P). Your court partner executes a medium-speed forehand drive to your forehand. Return this shot with a forehand cross-court volley. The ball must land in the target area defined by the service line, the singles sideline, the baseline, and the service divider line (extended) on your partner's backhand side (crosscourt from you) (see Illustration 5.3). If your partner's shot to you is not accurate, still make an attempt to hit it. If you are not successful on an errant shot, do not count that one. Practice this task in blocks of 10 shots. Record the number of successful shots for each block on the **Personal Recording Form**. When four block scores reach or exceed 7 out of 10 (they do not have to be consecutive), have your partner initial and date in the space provided.

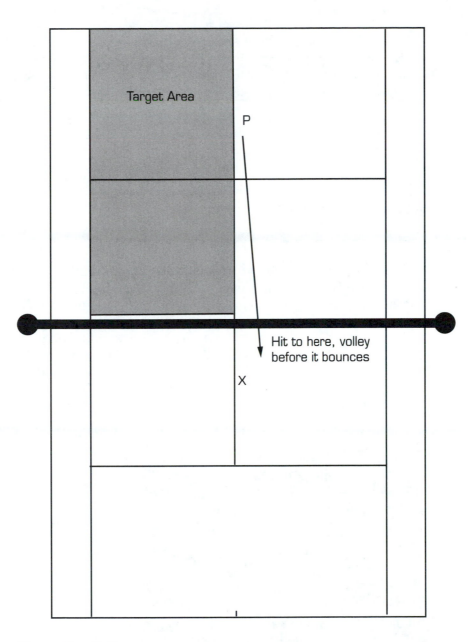

Target Area

P

Hit to here, volley
before it bounces

X

Illustration 5.3
Criterion Task 5-2

Personal Recording Form									
Block 1	Block 2	Block 3	Block 4	Block 5	Block 6	Block 7	Block 8	Block 9	Block 10
___/10	___/10	___/10	___/10	___/10	___/10	___/10	___/10	___/10	___/10

Your partner's initials _____ Date completed _____

BACKHAND VOLLEY

INSTRUCTOR DEMONSTRATION

Your course instructor will provide you with an explanation and demonstration of the key performance cues for the backhand volley shot. If you have questions, be sure to ask them before proceeding to the individualized task sequence. As you will note, the backswing and the follow-through are severely shortened, and top spin is not used. There is a premium on placement, not on speed or spin. The backhand volley involves three phases: **preparation** (preparing to stroke the ball), **contact** (contacting the ball) and **follow-through** (stroke pattern after ball contact). Refer to Photos 5.2A through C as your instructor explains and demonstrates each performance cue for the forehand drive.

Photo 5.2A
Backhand volley, preparation phase

Photo 5.2B
Backhand volley, contact phase

Photo 5.2C
Backhand volley, follow-through phase

PERFORMANCE CUES FOR PREPARATION PHASE
(note position on the court)

1. **Grip:** Continental one-hand backhand grip.
2. **Knees:** Slightly flexed, ready for a short, quick step in either direction.

PERFORMANCE CUES FOR CONTACT PHASE

3. **Weight transfer:** Forward toward front foot.
4. **Ball contact:** Even with or slightly forward of the front foot.

PERFORMANCE CUES FOR FOLLOW-THROUGH PHASE

5. **Body rotation:** Hip and shoulders rotate slightly toward the net.
6. **Forward swing:** Continues toward the net with a short follow-through.

COMPREHENSION TASK

Find a partner and demonstrate to each other the proper performance cues for the backhand volley shot *without hitting the ball.* Start out with slow, deliberate strokes. Be sure to provide feedback to each other for correct and incorrect performance cues until both of you can execute this shot correctly.

LEARNING TIPS

1. Always start from the ready position, close to the net.
2. Keep the elbows in close and slightly in front of the body.
3. Be ready to change your grip as soon as you decide which side to hit from.
4. The knees are flexed and the body weight is on the balls of the feet.
5. Immediately upon determining on which side the ball is approaching, use hip and shoulder rotation to initiate your body pivot.
6. Use very little backswing; no farther than even with the hitting shoulder.
7. Shift body weight from back to front as you initiate the forward swing.
8. The head of the racquet should be above the approaching ball as the racquet moves toward point of contact.
9. The forward swing is a punching or blocking motion. At the point of ball impact, keep the wrist **firm**.
10. The follow-through is relatively short (approximately 12 to 15 inches past ball impact).

READINESS DRILLS

5-4.   Find a spot in the practice area, facing a fence or hitting wall. Stand about 10 feet from the fence. While always starting from the ready position, bounce the ball to yourself and gently hit 50 backhand volley shots into the fence. Do not be concerned with a specific aiming area at this time. Use these shots to gauge the proper timing, feel, and contact point for this shot. *Remember, hit gentle shots.*

5-5.   Take a position near the net with your dominant side toward the net. Gently drop a ball onto the court on your backhand side. As the ball bounces from the court, stroke it over the net with a backhand volley. Your objective is to just get the ball over the net, landing anywhere in the opposite doubles court area. Do not be concerned with accuracy at this time. Do this until you have hit 50 successful backhand volleys.

5-6.   You will need a partner for this drill. Assume the ready position approximately 6 to 8 feet behind the net (X). Have your partner stand just inside the service line on the other side of the court, slightly off to your backhand side (P), and gently toss (underhand) balls to your backhand side. Move to the ball and stroke it before it hits the court. Your objective is to just get the ball over the net, landing anywhere in the opposite doubles court area (see Illustration 5.4). Do not be concerned with

hitting the ball hard at this time. Do this until you have hit 50 successful backhand volleys.

If you experience difficulty with the readiness drills, refer to the **Performance Cues** and review each cue as presented. If you still have difficulty, ask
your course instructor to assist you in applying these techniques.

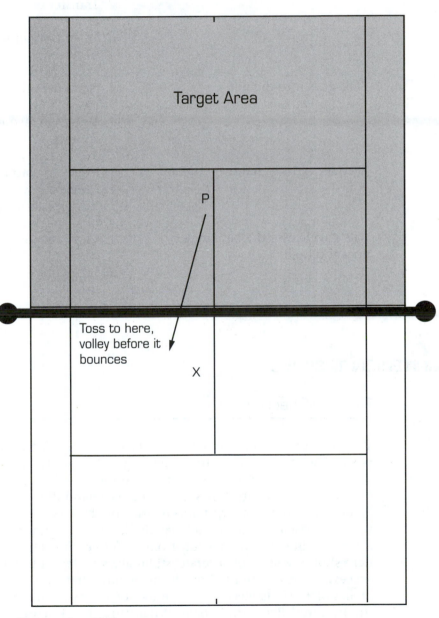

Illustration 5.4
Readiness Drill 5-6

Common Errors and Their Correction

Error	Correction
No power on the volleys.	1. Anticipate and be ready.
	2. Transfer body weight to front foot.
	3. Make contact just forward of front foot.
Balls goes into the net.	1. Flex knees to get your body low.
	2. Open the racquet face prior to contact.
Racquet turns in hand at contact.	1. Check for proper grip.
	2. Keep your wrist locked and firm through contact.
Ball travels over the baseline or goes too high.	1. Close face of the racquet at contact.
	2. Shorten the length of your stroke.

CRITERION TASK 5-3

Partner-Checked

Take a ready position close to the net (X). Have your court partner take a position across the net in the area between the service line and the baseline (P). Your court partner executes a medium speed forehand drive to your backhand side. Return this shot with a backhand down-the-line volley. The ball must land in the target area defined by the service line, the singles sideline, the baseline, and the service divider line (extended) on your partner's forehand side (directly upcourt from you) (see Illustration 5.5). If your partner's shot to you is not accurate, still make an attempt to hit it. If you are not successful on an errant shot, do not count that one. Practice this task in blocks of 10 shots. Record the number of successful shots for each block on the **Personal Recording Form**. When three block scores reach or exceed 7 out of 10 (they do not have to be consecutive), have your partner initial and date in the space provided.

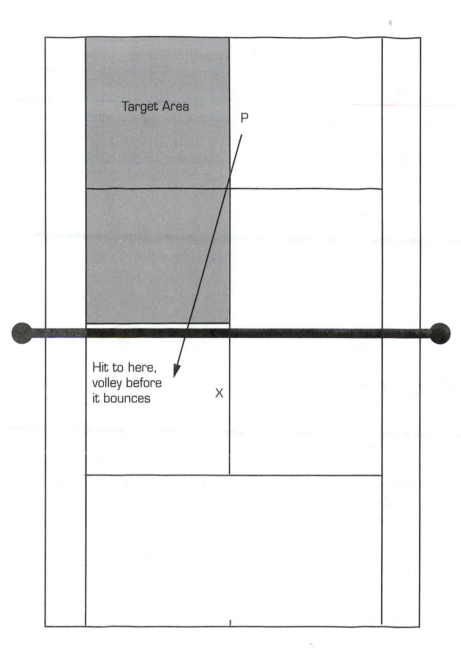

Target Area

P

Hit to here,
volley before
it bounces

X

Illustration 5.5
Criterion Task 5-3

Personal Recording Form									
Block 1	Block 2	Block 3	Block 4	Block 5	Block 6	Block 7	Block 8	Block 9	Block 10
__/10	__/10	__/10	__/10	__/10	__/10	__/10	__/10	__/10	__/10

Your partner's initials _____   Date completed _____

CRITERION TASK 5-4

Partner-Checked

Take a ready position close to the net, slightly to the left of the service divider line (X). Have your court partner take a position across the net in the area between the service line and the baseline (P). Your court partner executes a medium-speed forehand drive to your backhand side. Return his shot with a backhand crosscourt volley. The ball must land in the target area defined by the front service line, the singles sideline, the baseline, and the service divider line (extended) on your partner's backhand side (crosscourt from you) (see Illustration 5.6). If your partner's shot to you is not accurate, still make an attempt to hit it. If you are not successful on an errant shot, do not count that one. Practice this task in blocks of 10 shots. Record the number of successful shots for each block on the **Personal Recording Form**. When three block scores reach or exceed 7 out of 10 (they do not have to be consecutive), have your partner initial and date in the space provided.

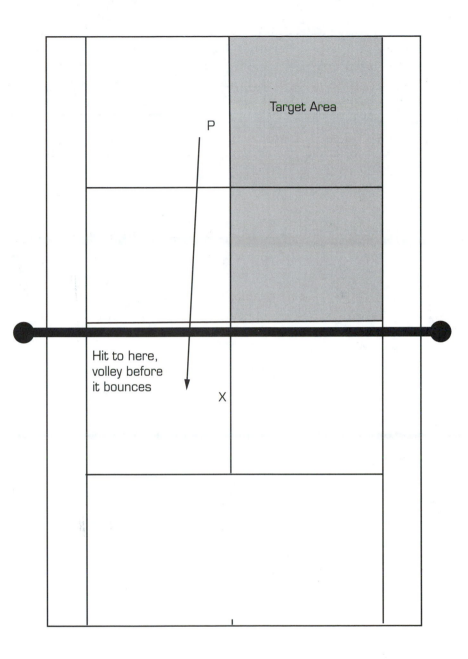

P

Target Area

Hit to here,
volley before
it bounces

X

Illustration 5.6
Criterion Task 5-4

Personal Recording Form									
Block 1	Block 2	Block 3	Block 4	Block 5	Block 6	Block 7	Block 8	Block 9	Block 10
___/10	___/10	___/10	___/10	___/10	___/10	___/10	___/10	___/10	___/10

Your partner's initials _____   Date completed _____

MODULE **6**

SERVING

INTRODUCTION

Every point in a tennis match begins with one player serving the ball to the opponent. Without a doubt, this is the most crucial strategic time in every point, because it is the only time when a player has complete control over the shot selected and the movement of the opponent. It is therefore extremely important that you spend a significant amount of time developing an effective serve. The service stroke pattern is complex when compared to forehand and backhand drives and volleys. It is a unique skill, like no other in tennis or any other sport, so even experienced athletes must start from scratch when learning it.

Because the server must hit the ball into a defined legal area or lose the point, the returner can predict when and where the ball will come to him or her. Therefore, it is important that you develop a service stroke that is accurate, powerful, and consistent, keeping your opponent off balance. Otherwise, you can lose the advantage of possessing the serve for an entire game.

INSTRUCTOR DEMONSTRATION

Your course instructor will provide you with an explanation and demonstration of the key performance cues for the full serve swing. If you have questions, be sure to ask them before proceeding to the individualized task sequence. The serve involves four phases: **preparation** (preparing to stroke the ball), **toss and backswing** (toss and backswing are nearly simultaneous), **contact** (contacting the ball), and **follow-through** (stroke pattern after ball contact). Refer to Photos 6.1A through E as your instructor explains and demonstrates each of the performance cues for the serve. As you will note, the serve involves many small parts, several of which happen simultaneously, accounting for the complexity of its description. It is actually much easier to execute than to describe, so don't be overwhelmed at first!

PERFORMANCE CUES FOR PREPARATION PHASE
(note position on the court)

1. **Grip:** Eastern forehand grip.
2. **Position:** Right behind baseline, near serving box divider marker, cross-court to intended service box.
3. **Alignment:** Front foot is 45 degrees past clockwise to aiming spot, left foot faces target spot.

Photo 6.1A
Serving preparation phase

Photo 6.1B
Toss phase

PERFORMANCE CUES FOR TOSS AND BACKSWING PHASE

4. **Grip on ball:** Cradle ball in nondominant hand; do not wrap fingers fully around the ball.
5. **Elbow:** Lock left elbow and lift from the shoulder, as if setting the ball on a shelf.
6. **Height:** The top of the toss should be just above your outstretched reach with the racquet.
7. **Placement:** About 24 inches in front of you, on line with front foot.
8. **Backswing:** Low sweeping action, then arm up to parallel with court.
9. **Weight shift:** Rocking action from front foot to back foot.

PERFORMANCE CUES FOR CONTACT PHASE

10. **Weight transfer:** Forward toward front foot.
11. **Ball contact:** In front, at apex of racquet reach.

Photo 6.1C
Backswing phase

Photo 6.1D
Serving contact phase

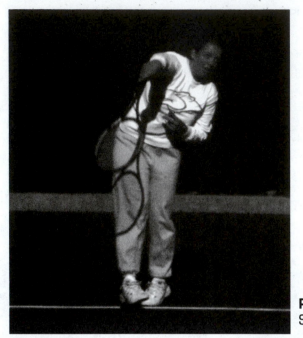

Photo 6.1E
Serving Follow-through phase

PERFORMANCE CUES FOR FOLLOW-THROUGH PHASE

12. **Wrist action:** Hard downward snap.
13. **Racquet:** Continues down and across the body.
14. **Hip rotation:** Hips rotate counterclockwise, bringing the right leg forward and across the baseline.
15. **Finish:** In ready position, just inside baseline.

COMPREHENSION TASK

Find a partner and demonstrate to each other the proper performance cues for the serve *without hitting the ball*. Start out with slow, deliberate strokes. Be sure to provide feedback to each other for correct and incorrect performance cues until both of you can execute the serve technique correctly.

LEARNING TIPS

1. The ball toss is a key component in serving. Extreme variation in the ball toss will force you to significantly alter your regular serving pattern and result in errant shots.
2. With this in mind, remember that the rules allow you to toss the ball and not attempt to hit it. So if you make an errant toss, simply do not swing at it.
3. The ball toss should be high enough for the point of contact to be made with the racquet in a fully extended position.
4. Think of your racquet traveling on one continuous, smooth path. Avoid jerky motions and stop—start movements that lose momentum
5. Execute a full follow-through. The racquet should be directed down in front of and across the body.
6. Always finish inside the baseline, in the ready position, in anticipation of your opponent's return shot to your side.

READINESS DRILLS

6-1.   Find a court line somewhere in the practice area. It does not have to be a baseline. Assume the proper stance for the serve, with an aiming area in mind. With chalk, mark a circle directly in line from your front foot, about 2 feet away. The circle should have a radius of 1 foot. This is your target. (You can also use an old tennis racquet for this, with the head as the target.) With one ball in your tossing hand and your racquet in

Photo 6.2A
Placement of target and toss

Photo 6.2B
Ball hitting in target

your hitting hand, practice tosses that go slightly above your out-stretched racquet and come down in the circle target. Do not hit the ball. Continue this drill until you make 25 accurate tosses. They do not have to be consecutive. Refer to Photos 6.2A and B.

6-2. Find a fence or wall space in the practice area. Make sure no one else is practicing near you. Assume the serving stance about 10 feet from the fence, facing it. Practice the full serve swing in **slow motion** by making tosses and hitting gentle serves into the fence. Do not be concerned with accuracy at this time. Do this until you have hit 50 successful serves.

6-3. Assume the serving stance right behind the **service line** on a court. Make sure no one else is practicing near you or hitting toward you. Practice the full serve swing in **slow motion** by making tosses and hitting gentle serves over the net and into the opposite doubles area. Do not be concerned with specific accuracy at this time. Concentrate on your toss, timing, contact, and follow-through to get a feel for this stroke. Do this until you have hit 50 successful serves.

Common Errors and Their Correction

Errors in the serve	Correction
Inconsistent ball flight.	1. Establish and use a set routine every time.
	2. Practice tossing accuracy more.
	3. Recognize errant tosses and do not attempt to hit them.
Ball goes over the baseline or pops up (wrist is ahead of your racquet at contact point).	Adjust the ball toss more to the front.
Ball goes into the net (wrist is behind your racquet at contact point).	Adjust the ball toss more to the back.
Ball curves excessively.	Snap your wrist straight down after contact.

CRITERION TASK 6-1

Self-Checked

Take a serving position just behind the baseline (X) and execute serves into the forehand receiving area. The ball must land in the proper receiving court area (see Illustration 6.1). "Let" serves can be taken over, "faults" count as misses. Practice this task in blocks of 10 shots. Record the number of successful shots for each block on the **Personal Recording Form**. When four block scores reach or exceed 7 out of 10 (they do not have to be consecutive), initial and date in the space provided.

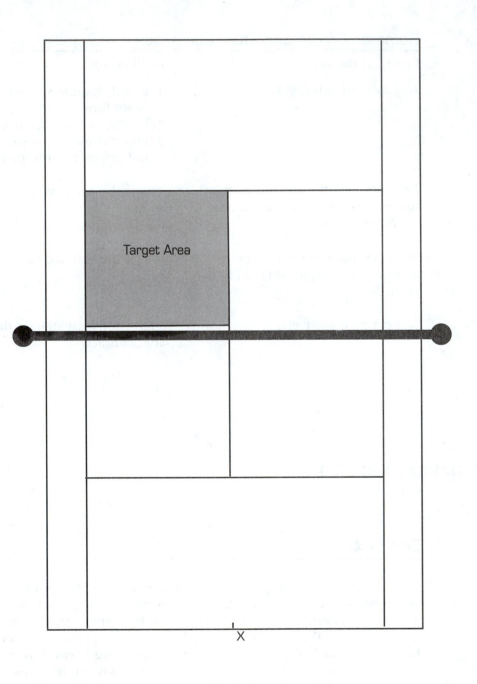

Illustration 6.1
Criterion Task 6-1

Personal Recording Form									
Block 1	Block 2	Block 3	Block 4	Block 5	Block 6	Block 7	Block 8	Block 9	Block 10
___/10	___/10	___/10	___/10	___/10	___/10	___/10	___/10	___/10	___/10

Your initials _____   Date completed _____

CRITERION TASK 6-2

Instructor-Checked

Use a cone or other marker to make a line 45 degrees off the opposite left baseline. The baseline and this line are called the *power line.* Take a serving position just behind the baseline to the right of serving mark (X). Execute serves into the forehand receiving area. **The ball must land in the receiving court area and then cross over the power line before the second bounce** (see Illustration 6.2). "Let" serves can be taken over; "faults" count as misses. Practice this task in blocks of 10 shots. Record the number of successful shots for each block on the **Personal Recording Form**. When your block scores consistently reach or exceed 7 out of 10, ask your instructor to witness and verify your mastery. This task is completed when your instructor has witnessed three blocks with a score of 7 or higher. The blocks do not have to be consecutive.

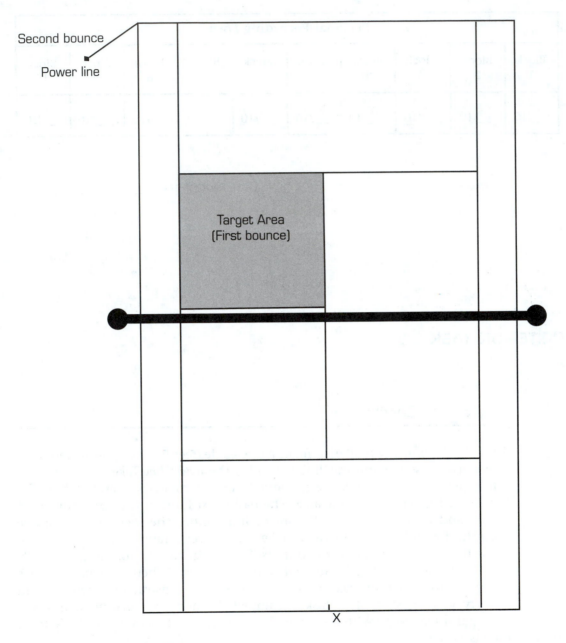

Second bounce

Power line

Target Area
(First bounce)

X

Illustration 6.2
Criterion Task 6.2

Personal Recording Form									
Block 1	Block 2	Block 3	Block 4	Block 5	Block 6	Block 7	Block 8	Block 9	Block 10
___/10	___/10	___/10	___/10	___/10	___/10	___/10	___/10	___/10	___/10

Your initials _____ Date completed _____

CRITERION TASK 6-3

Self-Checked

Take a serving position just behind the baseline to the left of the service mark (X) and execute serves into the backhand receiving area. The ball must land in the proper receiving court area (see Illustration 6.3). "Let" serves can be taken over; "faults" count as misses. Practice this task in blocks of 10 shots. Record the number of successful shots for each block on the **Personal Recording Form**. When four block scores reach or exceed 7 out of 10 (they do not have to be consecutive), initial and date in the space provided.

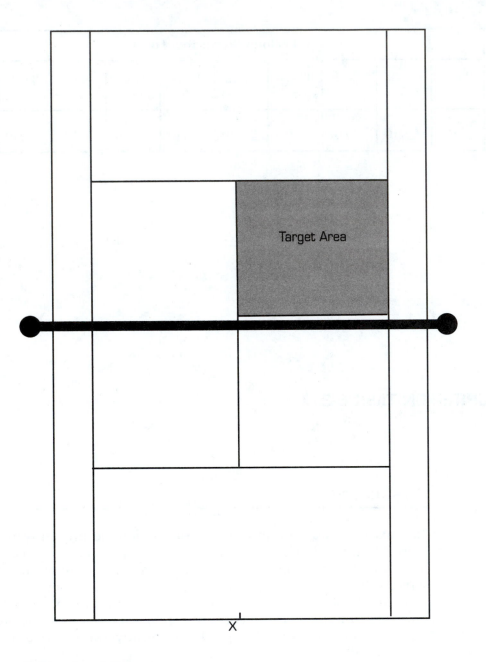

Target Area

X

Illustration 6.3
Criterion Task 6.3

Personal Recording Form									
Block 1	Block 2	Block 3	Block 4	Block 5	Block 6	Block 7	Block 8	Block 9	Block 10
___/10	___/10	___/10	___/10	___/10	___/10	___/10	___/10	___/10	___/10

Your initials _____   Date completed _____

CRITERION TASK 6-4

Instructor-Checked

Use a cone or other marker to make a line 45 degrees off the opposite right baseline. The baseline and this line are called the *power line*. Take a serving position just behind the baseline, to the left of the serving mark (X). Execute serves into the backhand receiving area. The ball must land in the receiving court area and then cross over the power line before the second bounce (see Illustration 6.4). "Let" serves can be taken over; "faults" count as misses. Practice this task in blocks of 10 shots. Record the number of successful shots for each block on the **Personal Recording Form**. When your block scores consistently reach or exceed 7 out of 10, ask your instructor to witness and verify your mastery. This task is completed when your instructor has witnessed three blocks with a score of 7 or higher. The blocks do not have to be consecutive.

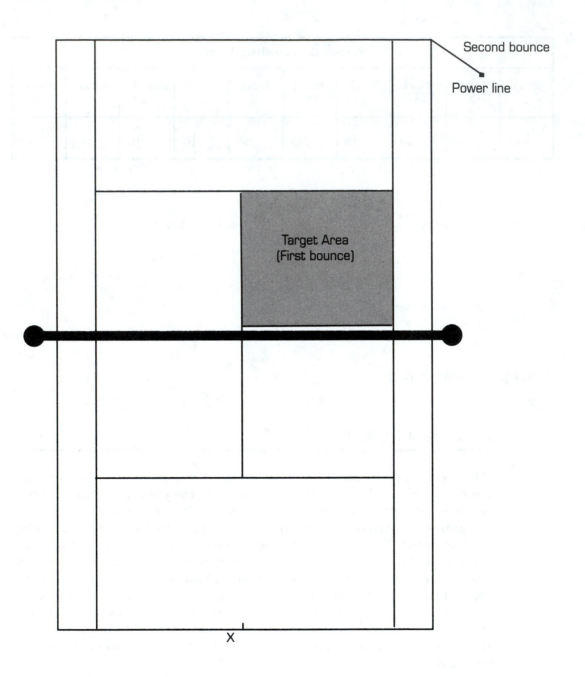

Second bounce

Power line

Target Area
(First bounce)

X

Illustration 6.4
Criterion Task 6.4

Personal Recording Form									
Block 1	Block 2	Block 3	Block 4	Block 5	Block 6	Block 7	Block 8	Block 9	Block 10
___/10	___/10	___/10	___/10	___/10	___/10	___/10	___/10	___/10	___/10

Your instructor's initials _____   Date completed _____

CHALLENGE TASK

Take a serving position behind the baseline. Have your court partner assume a receiving position on the opposite side of the court. Play a game with your court partner, using only the serve and the serve return. For every serve that lands in the target area, you receive 1 point. For each return of serve that lands in the singles court area, your partner receives 1 point. The server is allowed two serves to get the ball into play. Alternate serving to the forehand and backhand receiving areas. The first player to score 10 points wins the game. Switch serving and receiving roles after each game. To complete this task, you must play a total of two games.

MODULE 7

LOBS (OPTIONAL)

INTRODUCTION

If your opponent has gone to the net and established a position there, you have two options for your return shot. You can use a forehand or backhand passing shot, aimed between your opponent and the alley on the side you are hitting to. The techniques you used for forehand and backhand drives are used for the respective shot, so these are not new strokes to learn. The only difference is that you will aim for an alley. Your second option is to use a lob shot that carries over your opponent's head and lands deep in the opposite court, forcing her or him back to the baseline and out of attacking position.

FOREHAND LOB

The lob may be either an offensive or defensive shot. A good lob shot is disguised as a forehand or backhand drive with some slight changes in technique that can catch an aggressive opponent off guard at the net. The ball is stroked much like a drive shot, but with a lifting action and lots of top spin, making the return extremely difficult. An offensive lob shot is used to force your opponent into a difficult return or to allow you to approach the net when she or he is forced to the back of the court. A defensive lob is often used when a player is forced out of position and must "buy time" to regain court position as the opponent is forced to return the ball with an overhead smash.

Lobs shots can be hit with the forehand or backhand and have offensive or defensive strategic purposes. Because these are advanced shots, your PSIS tennis course will just introduce you to the basics of forehand and backhand lobs to help you develop your initial skill, with no distinction between offensive or defensive lob shots. If time permits, your instructor can provide you with specific applications for each lob shot once you have completed this module.

INSTRUCTOR DEMONSTRATION

Your course instructor will provide you with an explanation and demonstration of the key performance cues for the forehand lob. If you have questions, be sure to ask them before proceeding to the individualized task sequence. The forehand lob involves three phases: **preparation** (preparing to stroke the ball), **contact** (contacting the ball) and **follow-through** (stroke pattern after ball contact). Refer to Photos 7.1A through C as your instructor explains and demonstrates each of the performance cues for the forehand lob.

Photo 7.1A
Preparation phase

Photo 7.1B
Contact phase

Photo 7.1C
Follow-through phase

PERFORMANCE CUES FOR PREPARATION PHASE

1. **Grip:** Eastern forehand grip.
2. **Body position:** Nondominant side to the net, with knees flexed.
3. **Backward swing:** Racquet head is well below waist level.

PERFORMANCE CUES FOR CONTACT PHASE

4. **Wrist:** Firm at point of contact.
5. **Forward swing:** Lift the racquet into and through the ball.
6. **Body position:** Short forward step with knee extension.

PERFORMANCE CUES FOR FOLLOW-THROUGH PHASE

7. **Body position:** Body extends to fully upright position.
8. **Forward swing:** Follow-through upward and through the line of the ball.

COMPREHENSION TASK

Find a partner and demonstrate to each other the proper performance cues for the forehand lob *without hitting the ball*. Start out with slow, deliberate strokes. Be sure to provide feedback to each other for correct and incorrect performance cues until both of you can execute this shot correctly.

LEARNING TIPS

1. The recommended grip for the forehand lob is the Eastern. You can experiment with slightly different hand positioning to "customize" your grip for this shot.
2. Always start from the ready position and change to the proper grip before you begin your swing.
3. When you take the racquet back, make sure that your hips and shoulders rotate to position your side to the approaching ball.
4. When executing the foot pivot, shift your body weight to your rear foot.
5. Use a lifting, softer swing to prevent the ball from going over the opposite baseline.
6. Take a small step forward to contact the approaching ball and make sure your body weight shifts from back foot to front foot.
7. At the point of ball impact, keep the wrist firm to minimize vibration.

READINESS DRILLS

7-1.   Find a spot in the practice area, facing a fence or hitting wall. Stand about 4 to 6 feet from the fence. While always starting from the ready position, bounce the ball to yourself and gently hit 50 forehand lobs into the fence. Do not be concerned with a specific aiming area at this time. However, from this position you should not be lobbing the ball over the fence. Use these shots to gauge the proper timing, feel, and contact point for this shot. *Remember, hit gentle shots.*

7-2.   Take a position behind the baseline with your nondominant side toward the net (X). Gently drop a ball onto the court on your forehand side. As the ball bounces from the court, stroke it over the net with a forehand lob. Your objective is to get the ball over the net with a medium trajectory, landing anywhere in the opposite doubles court area (see Illustration 7.1). Do this until you have hit 50 successful forehand lobs.

7-3.   You will need a partner for this drill. Assume the ready position approximately 5 to 7 feet behind the baseline (X). Have your partner (P) stand close to the net on your side of the court and gently toss (underhand) balls to your forehand side. Move to the ball and stroke it on the first bounce with a forehand lob. Your objective is to get the ball over your partner's head and landing anywhere in the opposite doubles court area (see Illustration 7.2). Do this until you have hit 50 successful shots.

If you experience difficulty with the readiness drills, to the **Performance Cues** and review each cue as presented. If you still have difficulty, ask your course instructor to assist you in applying these techniques.

Common Errors and Their Correction

Error	Correction
The lob is not high enough to get over your opponent's head.	1. Make your lifting action more pronounced. 2. Shorten your front step.
The lob travels consistently over the opposite baseline.	1. Contact point is too high. 2. Rotate your wrist more on the follow-through to produce more top spin.

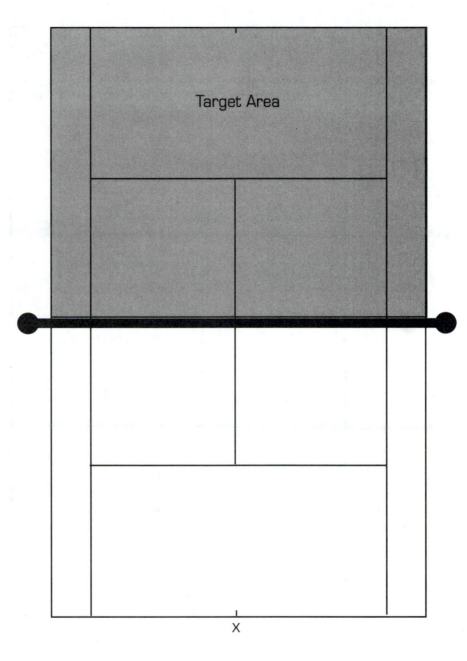

Illustration 7.1
Readiness Drill 7-2

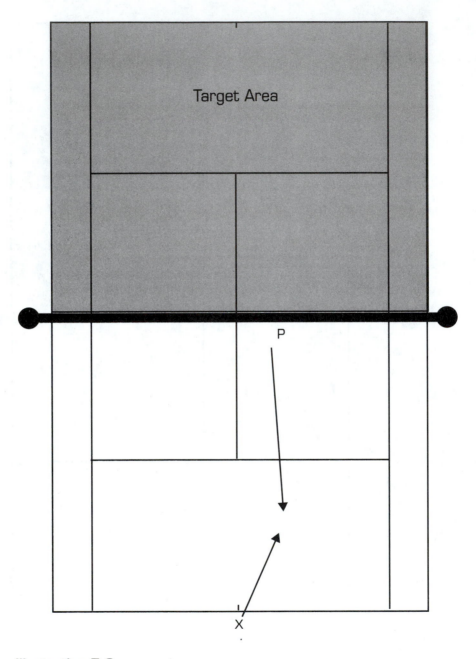

Illustration 7.2
Readiness Drill 7-3

CRITERION TASK 7-1

Partner-Checked

Assume a ready position just behind the baseline (X). Have your partner take a position directly across the net at the service line (P) and hit medium-paced shots to your forehand side. Once your partner hits the ball, she should raise his or her racquet over her head, providing you with the proper trajectory needed for your lob shots. The target area is defined by the back service line, the baseline, and the singles sidelines on the side of the opposite court that your partner is standing in (see Illustration 7.3). For a shot to count as successful, it must hit in the target area *and* go past your partner over the height of her outstretched racquet. If your partner's shot to you is not accurate, still make an attempt to hit it. If you are not successful on an errant shot, do not count that one. Practice this task in blocks of 10 shots. Record the number of successful shots for each block on the **Personal Recording Form**. When four block scores reach or exceed 7 out of 10 (they do not have to be consecutive), have your partner initial and date in the space provided.

Personal Recording Form									
Block 1	Block 2	Block 3	Block 4	Block 5	Block 6	Block 7	Block 8	Block 9	Block 10
___/10	___/10	___/10	___/10	___/10	___/10	___/10	___/10	___/10	___/10

Your partner's initials _____   Date completed _____

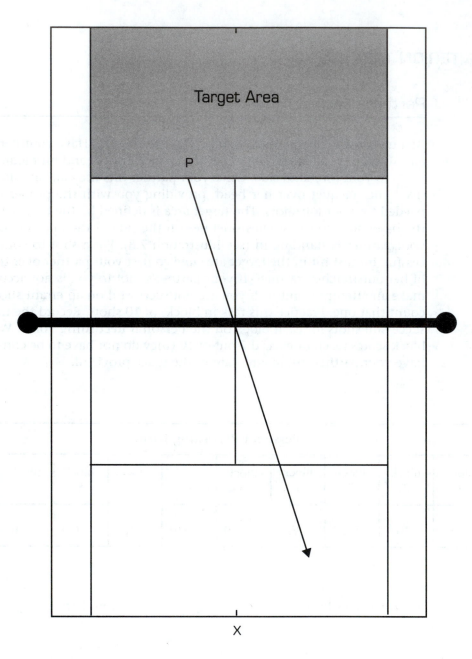

Illustration 7.3
Criterion Task 7-1

BACKHAND LOB

INSTRUCTOR DEMONSTRATION

Your course instructor will provide you with an explanation and demonstration of the key performance cues for the backhand lob. If you have questions, be sure to ask them before proceeding to the individualized task sequence. The backhand lob involves three phases: **preparation** (preparing to stroke the ball), **contact** (contacting the ball) and **follow-through** (stroke pattern after ball contact). Refer to Photos 7.2A through C as your instructor explains and demonstrates each performance cue for the backhand lob.

PERFORMANCE CUES FOR PREPARATION PHASE

1. **Grip:** Two-hand backhand grip.
2. **Body position:** Dominant side to the net, with knees flexed.
3. **Backward swing:** Racquet head is well below waist level.

Photo 7.2A
Preparation phase

Photo 7.2B
Contact phase

Photo 7.2C
Follow-through phase

PERFORMANCE CUES FOR CONTACT PHASE

4. **Wrist:** Firm at point of contact.
5. **Forward swing:** Lift the racquet into and through the ball.
6. **Body position:** Short forward step with knee extension.

PERFORMANCE CUES FOR FOLLOW-THROUGH PHASE

7. **Body position:** Body extends to fully upright position.
8. **Forward swing:** Follow-through upward and through the line of the ball.

COMPREHENSION TASK

Find a partner and demonstrate to each other the proper performance cues for the back lob *without hitting the ball*. Start out with slow, deliberate strokes. Be sure to provide feedback to each other for correct and incorrect performance cues until both of you can execute this shot correctly.

LEARNING TIPS

1. The recommended grip for the backhand lob is the two-hand backhand grip. Some players will elect to use a one-hand grip for this shot by simply taking their top hand off the racquet. You can experiment with slightly different hand positioning to "customize" your grip for this shot.
2. Always start from the ready position and change to the proper grip before you begin your swing.
3. When you take the racquet back, make sure that your hips and shoulders rotate to position your side to the approaching ball.
4. When executing the foot pivot, shift your body weight to your rear foot.
5. Use a lifting, softer swing to prevent the ball from going over the opposite baseline.
6. Take a small step forward to contact the approaching ball and make sure your body weight shifts from back foot to front foot.
7. At the point of ball impact, keep the wrist firm to minimize vibration.

READINESS DRILLS

7-4. Find a spot in the practice area, facing a fence or hitting wall. Stand about 4 to 6 feet from the fence. While always starting from the ready position, bounce the ball to yourself and gently hit 50 backhand lobs into the fence. Do not be concerned with a specific aiming area at this time. However, from this position, you should not be lobbing the ball over the fence. Use these shots to gauge the proper timing, feel, and contact point for this shot. *Remember, hit gentle shots.*

7-5. Take a position behind the baseline with your dominant side toward the net (X). Gently drop a ball onto the court on your backhand side. As the ball bounces from the court, stroke it over the net with a backhand lob. Your objective is to get the ball over the net with a medium trajectory, landing anywhere in the opposite doubles court area (see Illustration 7.4). Do this until you have hit 50 successful forehand drives.

7-6. You will need a partner for this drill. Assume the ready position just behind the baseline (X). Have your partner stand close to the net on your side of the court (P) and gently toss (underhand) balls to your backhand side. Move to the ball and stroke it on the first bounce with a backhand lob. Your objective is to get the ball over your partner's head and landing anywhere in the opposite doubles court area (see Illustration 7.5). Do this until you have hit 50 successful shots.

Target Area

X

Illustration 7.4
Readiness Drill 7-5

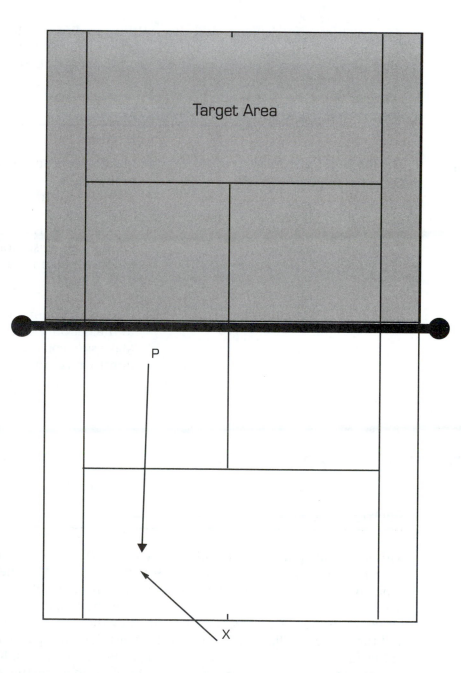

Illustration 7.5
Readiness Drill 7-6

If you are experiencing difficulty with the readiness drills refer to the **Performance Cues** and review each cue as presented. If you still have difficulty, ask your course instructor to assist you in applying these technique.

Common Errors and Their Correction

Error	Correction
The lob is not high enough to get over your opponent's head.	1. Make your lifting action more pronounced. 2. Shorten your front step.
The lob travels consistently over the opposite baseline.	1. Contact point is too high. 2. Rotate your wrist more on the follow-through to produce more top spin.
Ball goes too far right or left.	1. Have your dominant shoulder to the net on the backswing 2. Make sure you are stepping directly forward.

CRITERION TASK 7-2

Partner-Checked

Assume a ready position just behind the baseline (X). Have your partner take a position directly across the net at the service line (P) and hit medium-paced shots to your backhand side. Once your partner hits the ball, she should raise her racquet over her head, providing you with the proper trajectory needed for your lob shots. The target area is defined by the service line, the baseline, and the singles sideline on the side of the court that your partner is standing in (see Illustration 7.6). For a shot to count as successful, it must hit in the target area *and* go past your partner over the height of her outstretched racquet. If your partner's shot to you is not accurate, still make an attempt to hit it. If you are not successful on an errant shot, do not count that one.

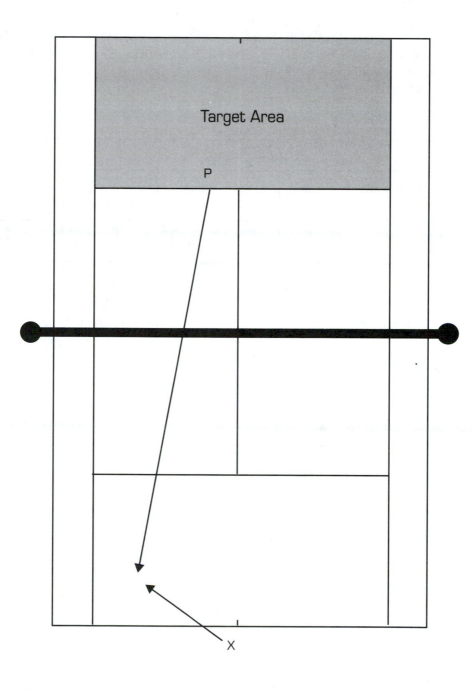

Illustration 7.6
Criterion Task 7-2

Practice this task in blocks of 10 shots. Record the number of successful shots for each block on the **Personal Recording Form**. When four block scores reach or exceed 7 out of 10 (they do not have to be consecutive), have your partner initial and date in the space provided.

Personal Recording Form									
Block 1	Block 2	Block 3	Block 4	Block 5	Block 6	Block 7	Block 8	Block 9	Block 10
___/10	___/10	___/10	___/10	___/10	___/10	___/10	___/10	___/10	___/10

Your partner's initials _____   Date completed _____

MODULE **8**

OVERHEAD SMASH (OPTIONAL)

INTRODUCTION

The overhead, often called a smash, is a stroke that is used to defend against the lob. A lob shot will typically produce a high bounce on your side of the court, allowing you to move under the ball and contact it well above your head with a strong downward pace. This is always an attacking shot and is used to win the point. Smashes can be made from any place on the court, but are much more effective the closer you set up to the net. The stroke pattern is similar to that of the serve. A player who plays an attacking game and approaches the net frequently must develop a strong smash. As with the serve, ball placement and pace are key attributes of an effective smash.

INSTRUCTOR DEMONSTRATION

Your course instructor will provide you with an explanation and demonstration of the key performance cues for the overhead smash. If you have questions, be sure to ask them before proceeding to the individualized task sequence. The overhead smash involves three phases: **preparation** (preparing to stroke the ball), **contact** (contacting the ball) and **follow-through** (stoke pattern after ball contact). As you will see, these shot mechanics are very similar to those of the serve. Refer to Photos 8.1A through C as your instructor explains and demonstrates each performance cue for the overhead smash.

Photo 8.1A
Smash preparation phase

Photo 8.1B
Smash contact phase

PERFORMANCE CUES FOR PREPARATION PHASE

1. **Grip:** Eastern forehand grip.
2. **Position:** Forty-five to ninety degrees facing the net, nondominant shoulder forward.
3. **Backswing:** A slightly abbreviated serving motion (do not "wind up")

PERFORMANCE CUES FOR CONTACT PHASE

4. **Forward swing:** Contact the ball in full body extension.
5. **Weight shift:** From rear foot to front foot, with short step.
6. **Ball contact:** In front of the body (to produce downward trajectory).

PERFORMANCE CUES FOR FOLLOW-THROUGH PHASE

7. **Wrist action:** Hard downward snap.
8. **Racquet:** Continues down and across the body.
9. **Hip rotation:** Hips rotate counterclockwise, bringing the right leg forward.

Photo 8.1C
Smash follow-through phase

COMPREHENSION TASK

Find a partner and demonstrate to each other the proper performance cues for the overhead smash without *hitting the ball*. Do not use a stationary position. Start from a ready position and move 3 to 4 steps in any direction to set up for each shot. Start out with slow, deliberate movement and strokes. Be sure to provide feedback to each other for correct and incorrect performance cues until both of you can execute this shot correctly.

LEARNING TIPS

1. Move quickly into proper court position to return the lob.
2. If the lob to you is very high, let it bounce once before executing the smash.
3. Align yourself directly behind the lob as it comes to your side so that you can move forward as you smash the ball.
4. Contact the ball with your body in full extension.
5. Follow through down and across your body, with a hard snap of the wrist.
6. Remember, this is a power shot, not an accuracy shot.

READINESS DRILL

8-1. Take a position behind the net close to the service line (X) and have your court partner stand across the net behind the baseline (P). Have your court partner hit slow-paced lobs directed toward your forehand court position. Move into position and hit 50 controlled overhead smashes that land anywhere in the opposite doubles court boundaries (see Illustration 8.1). Do not be concerned at first with hitting the ball hard. Use these shots to gauge the proper timing, feel, and contact point for this shot. *Remember, hit shots under control!*

Caution: Your partner must move out of the opposite court immediately after making his or her shot to avoid getting hit by your shot. If your partner does not move off the court, do not hit your shot.

Common Errors and Their Correction

Error	Correction
Hitting over the opposite baseline.	1. Position yourself well behind the lob so that you will be forced to move forward as you stroke the ball. 2. Make contact with the ball well forward of your body, forcing a downward motion.
Mishitting the ball (typically on the rim of the racquet).	1. Watch the ball as it comes to you, not your target. 2. This could be a timing problem caused by not getting fully under the ball to hit it.

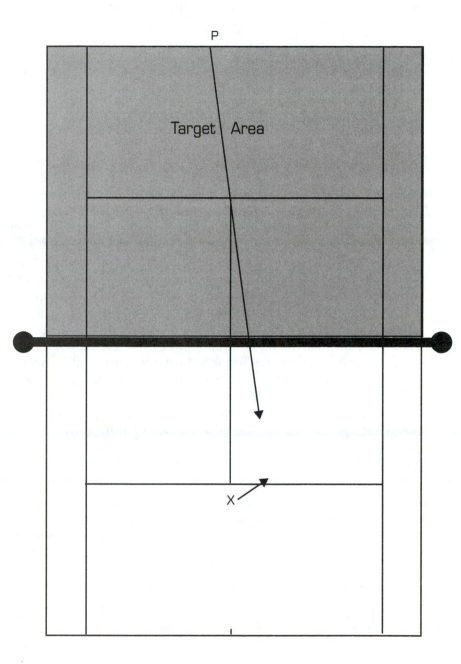

P

Target Area

X

Illustration 8.1
Readiness Drill 8-1

CRITERION TASK 8-1

Partner-Checked

Take a ready position between the service line and the baseline (X). Have your court partner take a position across the net in the area just inside the service line (P). Your court partner executes a medium-high lob to you so that it bounces near the service line. Return this shot with an overhead smash, either before or after it takes the first bounce. To be successful, your shot must land in the target area defined by the service line, the singles sideline, the baseline, and the service divider line (extended) on your partner's backhand side (crosscourt from you) (see Illustration 8.2). If your partner's shot to you is not accurate, still make an attempt to hit it. If you are not successful on an errant shot, do not count that one.

Caution: Your partner must move out of the opposite court immediately after making his/her shot to avoid getting hit by your shot. If your partner does not move off the court, do not hit your shot.

Practice this task in blocks of 10 shots. Record the number of successful shots for each block on the **Personal Recording Form.** When four block scores reach or exceed 7 out of 10 (they do not have to be consecutive), have your partner initial and date in the space provided.

Personal Recording Form									
Block 1	Block 2	Block 3	Block 4	Block 5	Block 6	Block 7	Block 8	Block 9	Block 10
___/10	___/10	___/10	___/10	___/10	___/10	___/10	___/10	___/10	___/10

Your partner's initials _____   Date completed _____

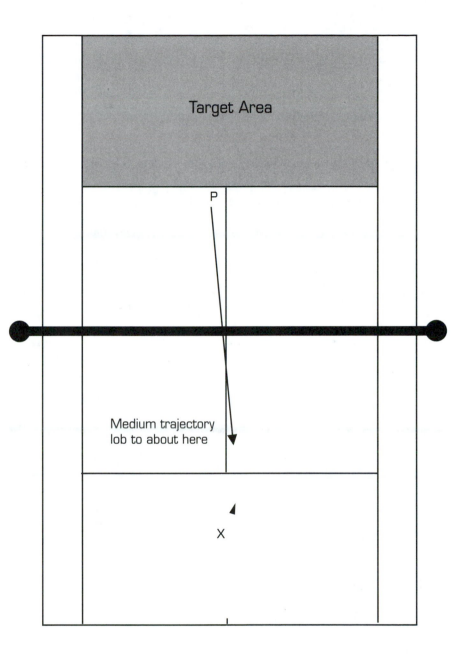

Illustration 8.2
Criterion Task 8-1

MODULE **9**

RULES OF TENNIS, STRATEGY, AND ETIQUETTE

INTRODUCTION

Having completed the skill performance modules of PSIS tennis, you are now ready to put them all together in match play against other players with comparable skill levels. As you will soon learn, the game of tennis is very fast-paced, requiring quick movements to the ball, split-second decisions, stamina, and keen strategy. To play the game for maximum enjoyment, you must first become familiar with its relatively simple rules, some basic strategy for singles and doubles play, and court etiquette. This module will help you with that learning.

READING ASSIGNMENT

Take time to carefully read the following sections on the Rules of Tennis, singles play, doubles play, and etiquette. As you read, make marginal notes on any items that are not clear to you. The next day in class ask your instructor to provide a longer explanation of these items or, better yet, a *demonstration*. Many of the rules and strategies can be best understood by seeing and hearing how they are interpreted and applied.

When you have finished the reading and have no more questions for your instructor, complete the brief Tennis Rules, Strategy and Etiquette Quiz in the back of this section. If the quiz will be used for grading, your instructor will inform you about how it will be evaluated. If this quiz will not be used for grading, it is recommended that you score at least 80% *and* have your instructor review missed answers with you. In this way you will have a good working knowledge of tennis before you begin competitive play in class or on your own.

RULES OF TENNIS*

SINGLES

Server and Receiver. The players stand on opposite sides of the net. The player who first delivers the ball is called the *server* and the other, the *receiver.*

Choice of Sides and Serve. The choice of sides and the right to be server or receiver in the first game is decided by toss. The player winning the toss may choose or require his or her opponent to (1) choose the right to be server or receiver, in which case the other player shall choose the side, or (2) choose the side, in which case the other player shall choose the right to be server or receiver.

Delivery at Service.   The service is delivered in the following manner: immediately before commencing to serve, the server positions him or herself with both feet at rest behind the baseline and within the imaginary continuation of the center mark and the sideline of the singles court. The server shall not serve until the receiver is ready. The server then throws the ball into the air in any direction and strikes it with her racket before it hits the ground. Delivery is deemed complete at the moment the racket strikes the ball.

Return of Service. The receiver may stand wherever he or she pleases on his or her own side of the net. However, he or she must allow the ball to hit the ground before returning service. If the receiver attempts to return the service, he or she shall be deemed ready.

Service from Alternate Courts. In delivering the service, the server stands alternately behind the right and left courts, beginning from the right in every game. The ball served shall pass over the net and hit the ground within the service court that is diagonally opposite or upon any line bounding such court before the receiver returns it. If the ball is erroneously served from the wrong half of the court, the resulting play stands, but service from the proper court, in accordance with the score, shall be resumed immediately after this discovery.

Faults. The service is a fault if the server misses the ball when attempting to serve it, if the ball does not land in the proper service court, or if the ball served touches a permanent fixture other than the net, strap, or band before it hits the ground. Throughout the delivery of the service, the server shall

Adapted with permission of the United States Tennis Association.

keep both feet behind the baseline and shall not change position by walking or running. A foot fault is called when the server steps on the baseline or into the court before his racquet meets the ball.

Service after a Fault. After a first fault, the Server again from behind the same half of the court from which he/she served that fault (unless it was a fault because he/she served from behind the wrong half, in which case he/she is entitled to deliver one service from behind the proper half).

A Service Let . During the service, a ball that touches the net but lands in the proper court is termed a let and counts for nothing. This one service is replayed. There is no limit to the number of let balls that may be made on the service; the server continues serving into the same court until a good service is delivered or two faults are made.

Receiver Becomes Server. At the end of the first game, the receiver becomes the server, and the server becomes the receiver, and so on alternately in all the subsequent games of the match. The players change sides at the end of the first, third and every subsequent alternate game. If a player serves out of turn, the player who ought to have served shall serve as soon as the mistake is discovered. All points scored before such discovery shall stand. If a game has been completed before such discovery, the order of service remains as altered.

Server Wins Point. The server wins the point if the ball served, not being a let, touches the receiver or anything that he or she wears or carries before it hits the ground or if the receiver otherwise loses the point, as described below.

Receiver Wins Point. The receiver wins the point if the server serves two consecutive faults or otherwise loses the point, as described below.

Ball Falling on Line Is Good. A ball falling on a line is regarded as falling in the court bounded by that line.

Player Loses Point. A player loses the point if:
1. He or she fails to return the ball in play directly over or past the end of the net before it has hit the ground twice consecutively.
2. He or she returns the ball in play so that it hits the ground, a permanent fixture (other than the net, posts or singles sticks, cord or metal cable, strap or band) or other objects outside any of the lines that bound his opponents court.
3. He or she deliberately carries or catches the ball in play on his racquet more than once.

4. He or she or the racquet touches the net, post, or ground within the opponent's court at any time while the ball is in play.
5. He or she volleys the ball before it has passed the net.
6. He or she volleys the ball and fails to make a good return even when standing outside the court.
7. He or she throws the racquet at and hits the ball.
8. He or she deliberately and materially changes the shape of the racquet during the playing of the point.
9. He or she deliberately commits any act that hinders his or her opponent in making a stroke.
10. The ball in play touches him or her or anything that he or she wears or carries other than the racquet in his hand.

A Good Return.   It is a good return if:
1. The ball touches and passes over the net, posts, cord or metal cable, strap or band and hits the ground within the court.
2. The ball touches any other permanent fixture after it has hit the ground within the proper court.
3. The ball hits the ground within the proper court and rebounds back over the net, and the player whose turn it is to strike reaches over the net and plays the ball, provided that neither she nor any part of his/her clothes or racquet touches the net, and that the stroke is otherwise good.
4. The ball is returned from outside the post, provided that it hits the ground within the proper court.
5. A player's racquet passes over the net after the player has properly returned the ball.
6. A player succeeds in returning a ball that has struck another ball lying in the court.

A Let.   In all cases where a let (other than a service let) has to be called under the rules to provide for an interruption of play, the point shall be replayed.

   If a player is hindered in making a stroke by anything not within his or her control, except a permanent fixture or deliberate interference by the opponent, a let shall be called.

Coaching.   A player may not receive coaching during the playing of any match other than one that is part of a team competition.

DOUBLES

The above rules apply to the doubles game except as described next.

Delivery of Service. The server positions both feet at rest behind the baseline and within the imaginary continuation of the center mark and the sideline of the doubles court.

Order of Service. At the beginning of each set, the pair serving the first game decides which partner shall do so and the opposing pair decides similarly for the second game. The partner of the player who served in the first game serves in the third; the partner of the player who served in the second game serves in the fourth, and so on, in the same order in all subsequent games of a set.

Order of Receiving. The pair receiving the service in the first game of each set decides which partner shall receive in the right-hand court, and the opposing pair decides similarly in the second game of each set. Partners receive the service alternately throughout each game. The order of receiving the service shall not be altered during the set, but may be changed at the beginning of a new set.

Service out of Turn. If a partner serves out of turn, the partner who ought to have served shall serve as soon as the mistake is discovered, but all points scored and any faults served before such discovery shall stand. If a game has been completed before such discovery, the order of service remains as altered.

Receiving out of Turn. If during a game the order of receiving the service is changed by the receivers, it remains as altered until the end of the game, but the partners shall resume their original order of receiving in the next game of that set in which they are the receivers.

Served Ball Touching Player. The service is a fault if the ball touches the server's partner or anything that the partner wears or carries. The server wins the point if the ball served (not being a let) touches the partner of the receiver or anything the partner of the receiver wears or carries before it hits the ground.

Ball Struck Alternately. The ball shall be struck by one or the other player of the opposing pairs in the course of making a serve or a return. If both of them hit the ball, either simultaneously or consecutively, their opponents win the point.

SCORING

A Game. If a player wins his or her first point, the score is called 15 for that player; on winning the second point, the score is called 30, on winning the third point, his score is called 40; and the fourth point won by a player is scored a game for that player except as follows:

If both players have won 3 points, the score is called *deuce*; the next point won by a player is scored *advantage* for that player. If the other player wins the next point, the score is again called *deuce;* and so on, *until a player wins the two points immediately following the score at deuce*, when the game is scored for that player.

A Set. A player (or players) who first wins six games wins a set, except that the player (or players) must win by a margin of two games over the opponent(s). Where necessary, a set is extended until this margin is achieved unless a tie-break system of scoring has been announced in advance of the match.

The players change sides at the end of the first, third, and every subsequent alternate game of each set and at the end of each set unless the total number of games in such set is even, in which case the change is not made until the end of the first game of the next set. The maximum number of sets in a match is five for men and three for women.

The Tie-break. If announced in advance of the match, a tie-break game operates when the score reaches six games all in any set. In singles, a player who first wins 7 points wins the game and the set provided he or she leads by a margin of 2 points. If the score reaches 6 points all, the game is extended until this margin has been achieved. Numerical scoring is used throughout the **tie-break game.** The player whose turn it is to serve is the server for the first point. Thereafter, each player serves in rotation for 2 points, in the same order as determined previously in that set, until the winners of the game and set have been decided.

From the first point, each service is delivered alternately from the right and left court, beginning from the right court. The first server serves the first point from the right court; the second server serves the second and third points from left and right court, respectively; the next server serves the fourth and fifth points from the left and right courts, respectively, and so on.

Players change ends after every 6 points and at the conclusion of the **tie-break game**. The player (or doubles pair) who served in the **tie-break game** shall receive service in the first game of the following set.

BASIC STRATEGY FOR SINGLES PLAY

1. Know your strengths and *play to them*. Every tennis player does certain things well and is better on some types of shots than others. This is called *knowing your game*. Once you have learned the strongest parts of your game, try to hit shots to your opponent that will force him or her into hitting back to your strengths. For example, if you have a good overhead smash shot, force your opponent to hit lob shots that you can return with smashes.

2. Know your opponent's strengths and *play away from them*. Like you, your opponent will want to force you to play to his or her strengths. Once you are aware of these strengths, hit more shots that force him or her to use weaker shots back to you.

3. Make your opponent move. Tennis matches can be long and tiring, so the player with the most stamina is often the winner. You can cause your opponent to become fatigued faster by using a variety of shot placements, forcing him or her to move around the court more.

4. Use aggressive shots to control the court. There is a great advantage to staying at the baseline in the middle of the court. You will have more choices for shots from that position. Conversely, you need to force your opponent out of that same area on his or her side. This is done by using controlled, aggressive shots that make your opponent move laterally and backward on his or her side. This will keep your opponent off balance and forced to make mostly defensive shots to you.

5. Be accurate with your serves. You surrender the point to your opponent automatically if you can not make two legal serves in a row. Develop one serve technique that gives you the most accuracy so that you can trust it for second serves, avoiding double faults.

6. Change the pace and placement of your serves. Even hard serves will not be effective if they are always hit with the same pace and to the same place. Your opponent will eventually adapt to this pattern and be ready for your serve, placing you on the defensive. Be sure to hit serves to your opponent's backhand side as often as possible.

7. Always stay in the point. The best tennis players do not give up when it appears they have lost the point being played. Some points can have long rallies with several momentum shifts in which one player has the advantage at a given moment, only to have the other player take back the advantage.

BASIC STRATEGY FOR DOUBLES PLAY

Tennis singles and doubles are two very different versions of the game, especially with highly skilled players. Doubles play relies less on serving and much more on volleying and net play. It is a very fast game, with the ball changing sides of the net quickly during long rallies.

1. Decide how your team will defend its side of the net, based on your abilities. The rules dictate which player will receive for your team to start the point. Once the served has been returned, you can choose any scheme you wish for defending your side of the court. Two schemes are used most often: *side by side* and *front and back*. In side by side, each player covers one side of the court, divided by the center service line (and extended). It is a good strategy to put your best backhand player on that side, to protect the alley. In front and back, one player covers the whole net area, while the other player covers the whole baseline. The player at the net needs good volleying skills, while the player at the back should have good groundstrokes. Photos 9.1 through 9.3 show the basic serving and defensive positions for doubles play.

Photo 9.1
Serving positions for doubles

Photo 9.2
Side-by-side defensive position

Photo 9.3
Front-and-back defensive position

2. Whichever way you choose, communicate between partners. The best player to return most shots will be obvious, but you can expect to get a number of "between" shots that go to the seam of your coverage areas, making it difficult to know who should make the return. There are no set rules for determining who should take a seam shot; both partners must be quick and decisive in making the choice and telling it to each other.

3. Hit shots directly at an opponent, to a seam, or up an alley. Much of the court is covered in doubles, so shots must be precise. It is acceptable to hit shots that go directly at an opponent, attempting to "handcuff" him or her into an awkward return. At the same time you must be careful not to aim these shots above an opponent's chest. When you know how your opponents are covering their court, the best attacking shots are those aimed at a seam between coverage areas. Other vulnerable areas are the alleys on each side, since many doubles teams tend to guard the center of the court more closely.

4. Be ready! Tennis doubles is a very fast game, with many long rallies and lots of volleying. You must always have your racquet in position for a return and your feet moving to execute proper footwork.

5. Sometimes just hit it "any way you can." The rapid pace in doubles, particularly in net play, can sometimes call for you to hit the ball in whatever way you can to make the return. Proper technique does not get tossed out the window, but at times you might have to improvise to make the shot you need.

TENNIS ETIQUETTE

The sport of tennis has a long tradition of promoting positive competition between players and teams. Several long-standing rules govern players' behavior during matches. Some of these rules are written into the rule book itself, and players are punished when rules are violated. Other rules are simply unwritten codes that make the game more enjoyable for players and spectators alike. Some of these items are under the referee's jurisdiction in an official match, but most often it is up to all players to referee their own matches in recreational settings.

1. Call the lines on your side of the court only. When there is no match referee, both players and teams are on an honor system to makes line calls *on their side of the court only*. The ball moves very fast, and sometimes a player does not see it clearly when it lands, but it is still his or her responsibility to make the call. It is often a good idea to agree before the match begins. to play over any disputed points.

2. The same goes for lets and net serves. Call only the shots that fall on your side of the net. Be clear and decisive so that your opponent knows the call you have made.

3. Play through close calls. At times you will not recognize that your opponent's serve or shot is "out" and you will strike the ball to return it simultaneously with making the call. Both players should get in the habit of playing all close shots in case they are good. If you hit a shot that you think is out on the other side, but is in fact good, you must still be ready to play it on the return. Saying "I thought my shot was out, so I stopped" is not a good strategy or an acceptable reason to replay the point

4. Always check that the receiver is ready before you serve. The rules cover instances when the service receiver is not ready, but it is good etiquette to give him or her adequate time to get into receiving position before you serve. The easiest way is to clearly call the score and allow 1 or 2 seconds to go by before making the toss. If the receiver is not ready, or wishes to question the score, he or she has enough time to make that indication.

5. The server calls the score before each point, always giving his or her score first.

6. If you are not ready as the receiver, simply don't attempt to hit the ball. According to the rules, if you attempt to hit a coming serve, you have indicated you are ready. The best thing to do is just not swing at it.

7. Do not toss your racquet or hit it on the court, net, or posts. Tennis can be a game of strong emotions, particularly during long rallies and key points. Frustration can sometimes prompt a player to toss the racquet or strike the court, net or posts with it. Even though this will likely hurt only the offending player and his or her racquet, it can be distracting to other player, and in extreme cases, lead to their injury.

8. Always respect your opponents, teammates, and yourself. Not every match will have players or teams with matching experience or abilities, resulting in an unfair competition. Some doubles teams will not have players of equal ability as well. When you are the more skilled player, you should not belittle your opponents or teammates with negative verbal comments and body language. The same goes for yourself when you are the lesser skilled player; no one likes to be on the court with someone who is overly self-critical in public.

TENNIS RULES, STRATEGY, AND ETIQUETTE QUIZ

Name _____ Date _____

Circle the letter that corresponds to the correct answer to each item.

1. The player winning the toss may choose or require his or her opponent to choose:
    A. the right to be the server
    B. the right to be the receiver
    C. the side
    D. any of the above

2. The serve is complete
    A. when the ball is tossed into the air
    B. the moment the racquet strikes the ball
    C. when the ball crosses the net
    D. when the ball strikes the opponent's court

3. The receiver must
    A. return the serve before the ball strikes the court
    B. return the serve on the first bounce
    C. assume a ready position behind the baseline
    D. assume a ready position outside the alley

4. It is a foot fault if the server
    A. misses the ball when attempting to serve it
    B. steps over the baseline before his or her racquet contacts the ball
    C. steps into the playing court before his or her racquet contacts the ball
    D. changes his/her position by walking or running into the service motion

5. The score is 30 to 15. During the next rally, the server's racquet touches the net when he or she is executing a volley. The score is now
    A. 30 to 15
    B. 30 to 30
    C. 40 to 15
    D. 15 to 30

6. The score is 15 to 30. During the next rally, the receiver volleys a ball before it passes over the net. The score is now
   A. 15 to 40
   B. 15 to 30
   C. 30 to 30
   D. Game

7. The score is 30 to 30. During the next rally a stray ball rolls onto the playing court and the server calls a let. The score is now
   A. 30 to 30
   B. 30 to 40
   C. 40 to 30
   D. 15 to 30

8. In a doubles match the score is love to 15. During the second serve the ball touches the partner of the server before entering the required receiving court. The receiver returns the serve into the net. The score is now
   A. 15 to 15
   B. love to 30
   C. 15 to 15 (first serve)
   D. 15 to 15 (second serve)

9. In a doubles match the score is 30 to 30. The server double faults. The score is now
   A. 30 to 30
   B. Serving team's advantage
   C. Receiving team's advantage
   D. 30 to 40

10. A player (or players) who first wins six games wins a set, except when the margin is
    A. one game
    B. two games
    C. three games
    D. four games

11. A serve that hits the net and then bounces into the proper serving area is called a
    A   fault, and not played over
    B. let serve, and is played over
    C. point for the server
    D. point for the receiver

12. When can a player's racquet touch the net without a penalty?
    A. Once the ball has entered his or her side of the court
    B. On the follow-through of an otherwise legal shot
    C. Never
    D. When he or she has slipped into the net

13. If you want to increase your chances of having your next shot be an overhead smash, you should hit a _____ to your opponent.
    A. deep lob
    B. forehand drive
    C. backhand drive
    D. volley

14. Which shot would you use to set up the opportunity to go to the net?
    A. Serve
    B. Forehand drive
    C. Backhand drive
    D. Approach shot

15. To which side of the receiver should you most often serve?
    A. Forehand
    B. Backhand

16. Doubles play will likely have more of which kinds of shots in it?
    A. Overhead smashes
    B. Volleys
    C. Approach shots
    D. Drive shots

17. A tie-break game is played when the set score becomes
    A. 6 to 4
    B. 6 to 5
    C. 6 to 6

18. You are the server. It is good etiquette to announce your opponent's score first to begin each point.
    A. True
    B. False

19. What are the two most common ways to cover your side of the court in doubles? (Must have both correct answers)
    A. Side by side
    B. Diagonal
    C. "First come, first hit"
    D. Front and back

20. It is a fault if the server tosses the ball and then does not attempt to strike it.
    A. True
    B. False

Personal Progress Chart for PSIS Tennis

Module		1	2	3	4	5	6	7	8	9	10	11	12	13	14	15
9	Rules, Strategy, Etiquette															
8	Overhead Smash (Optional)															
7	Lobs (Optional)															
6	Serving															
5	Volleys															
4	Approach Shots															
3	Ground Strokes															
2	Tennis Basics															
1	Stretching															
	Weeks in Class	1	2	3	4	5	6	7	8	9	10	11	12	13	14	15